SELECTED SONGS OF THOMAS CAMPION

Selected Songs of
THOMAS CAMPION

Selected and Prefaced by
W·H·AUDEN
Introduction by
JOHN HOLLANDER

DAVID GODINE · PUBLISHER · BOSTON · 1973

The punctuation and numbering of the songs herein follow the text of *The Works of Thomas Campion* by Walter R. Davis (1967). The calligraphy by Edith McKeon Abbott is based on music and texts in the editions of Fellowes and Davis. The facsimiles are printed with the permission of the Houghton Library, Harvard University, and the Folger Shakespeare Library, Washington D. C.

Copyright © 1972 by David R. Godine · Boston, Massachusetts.

LCC 71-152794
ISBN 0-87923-037-1 (deluxe)
0-87923-036-3 (trade)

PRINTED IN ITALY

CONTENTS

1564	John Campion married the widow of Roger Trigg.
1567 (February 12)	Thomas Campion born.
1576	John Campion died.
1577	Mother married Augustine Steward.
1579	Mother died.
1580	Stepfather remarried.
1581-84	Peterhouse College, Cambridge (did not take degree).
1586	Admitted to Gray's Inn, but was never called to the Bar.
1591	First English poem published. Probably took part in the Earl of Essex's expedition to Dieppe.
1593	Referred to by George Peele as one "that richly cloth'st conceits with well made words."
1595	Book of Latin poems published.
1601	*A Book of Ayres* (with Philip Rosseter).
Between 1602-1606	Qualified as a physician.
1605	Listed by Camden, along with such names as Sidney, Spenser, Drayton, Chapman, and Shakespeare, as one of the "most pregnant witts of these our times, whom succeeding ages may justly admire."
1615	Gave evidence at the enquiry into the Overbury murder case.
1620 (March 1)	Died.

[7]

PREFACE

THOMAS CAMPION is the only man in English cultural history who was both a poet and a composer. (Rather oddly, there seems to be no record of where or how he received a professional musical education.) Tom Moore was also a musician, but he wrote his songs for traditional Irish tunes, even if he may sometimes have modified them. Campion's songs can, of course, be enjoyed as spoken verse without their music, but they would not be what they are or sound as they do if he had not, when he wrote them, been thinking in musical terms. Again, if one forgets that he was a composer, one is tempted to write off his *Observations in the Art of English Poesie* as just one more wrongheaded attempt of a humanist to "classicize" English poetry. It is true that, in theory, he condemns rhyme as barbarous, but, in practice, aside from the examples he gives in the book – which are, by the way, much better than earlier generations thought them – he wrote only one unrhymed poem, the *Sapphics* of *A Book of Ayres, XXI*. Even in so classical an experiment as *Canto Secundo*, the asclepiadians are rhymed. Again in his *Masques*, one would have expected the speeches to be in blank verse, the one unrhymed form which has always been found acceptable in English poetry – but in fact, he always rhymed them. If he took more pride in his Latin poems than his English, which he called "superfluous blossoms of my deeper studies," nobody who knows anything about poets will take this too seriously. All he probably meant was, firstly, that he found writing Latin verses more difficult and, secondly, that he knew very few of his contemporary poets who could write them at all.

The real significance of Campion's *Observations* is that a poet writing in English need not think about vowel length,

[9]

only about stress. A composer, no matter what language he is setting, must think about both.

Though we have no proof, I feel reasonably certain that the prosodic principles of Greek and Latin poetry, in which one long syllable is regarded as equivalent to two short syllables, and a syllable, short in itself, becomes long when followed by more than one consonant, were derived from music. When I was a boy and, in Campion's time, too, I imagine, the rhythms of Latin verse were not understood by the English, for we simply stressed the long syllables which, in fact, meant treating all syllables as of equal length. For example, we recited the first half line of the *Aeneid* thus:

Árma virúmque canó

Musically, this is in waltz time, and the first two feet are not, quantitatively, dactyls as they should be, but tribrachs.

The quantitatively correct musical setting is in march time.

Because of the secondary beat in a musical bar, this means that quantitative dactyls, if scanned by stress, become bacchics. In fact, the musical rhythms of an accentual prosody are the reverse of a quantitative one. In English, as Campion realized, it is iambic or trochaic verse that is in march time. Then, though he does not, I believe, discuss it, he must have known, as a composer, that when sung at slow tempi, words can change their metrical value. Thus, when spoken, the line

O sacred head sore wounded

is iambic or trochaic: but, when sung to Bach's chorale, it becomes spondaic.

In my opinion, Campion is the greatest master in English poetry of what the French symbolists called *la poésie pure*. If I have to admit that he is, nevertheless, a minor poet, this is because I believe that "major" poetry is, necessarily, "impure." What he has to offer us is a succession of verbal paradises in which almost the only element taken from the world of everyday reality is the English language. Since words, unlike musical notes, are denotative, his songs have to be "about" some topic like love or religion, but the topic is not itself important. As C. S. Lewis has written:

> *His poetry is as nearly passionless as great poetry can be. There are passions somewhere in the background, but a passion, like a metre, is to Campion only a starting point: not for moral or intellectual activity but for the creation of a new experience which could occur only in poetry. By the time he has finished, the original, the merely actual, passion hardly survives as such: it has all been used. This happens as much in his religious as in his erotic pieces.*

For this reason, I cannot imagine a translation of his poems into another tongue which would have any value or meaning whatsoever. Change the sound of a syllable or the rhythm of a line, and all is lost. To explain what I mean, let me try to analyze four stanzas.

1. In Myr/tle Ar/bours on/ the downes/   (8)   a
       The Fai/rie Queen / Proser/pina,   (8)   x
   This night / by moone/-shine lead/ing
       merr/ie rounds   (10)   a
       Holds a watch / with sweet love,   (6)   b
   Down the dale, / up the hill; /   (6)   c
       No plaints / or groans / may move /   (6)   b
   Their holy / vigill.   (5)   c

Lines 1, 2, 3, and 6 are straightforward iambics, but variety is provided by the varying number of feet, 4, 4, 5 and 3, and the much lighter final stress of *Proserpina* compared with *downes*, *rounds*, and *move*. Also, this line is a refrain which occurs in every stanza and does not rhyme. Lines 4 and 5 are linked by metre – each consists of two cretics – but not by rhyme. Though, in isolation from the other stanzas, one would be inclined to scan line 7 as

> Their ho/ly vig/ill

after looking at the other stanzas, I think Campion means us to read it as an adonic.

2. Fountain/of health, / my soules / deepe
          wounds / recure   (10)   a
    Sweet showres / of pit/ty raine, / wash my /
          unclean / nesse pure.   (12)   a
      One drop / of thy desir/ed grace   (8)   b
    The faint / and fad/ing heart / can raise, /
          and in / ioyes be / some place   (14)   b
      Sinne and Death, / Hell and temp/ting
          Fiends / may rage;   (10)   c
    But God / his own / will guard / and their /
          sharp paines / and griefe / in time /
          asswage   (16)   c

Lines 4 and 6 are in regular iambics but of different lengths. In line 1, Campion inverts the first foot, and in line 2 the fourth. Line 3 *can* be read as four iambs but, since in the first stanza the corresponding line runs

> Lord light me to thy blessed way

I think that Campion probably means us to scan it as a spondee, a choriamb and an iamb. In line 5, something occurs which is very rare in spoken verse, but not infrequent in musical setting: the first two feet are molossoi.

3. All my desire, / all my delight / should be,
    Her to enioy, / her to unite / to mee:
    Envy should cease, / her would I love / alone:
    Who loves / by lookes, / is sel/dome true / to one.

Heroic couplets are one of the commonest verse forms in English, but Campion gives them a completely new movement in the first three lines by inverting the first and the third foot, so that they scan as two choriambs followed by an iamb.

4. The lov/ers teares / are sweet, / their mov/er
            makes / them so;   (12)
    Proud of / a wound / the blee/ding Sould/iers   (10)
            grew (10)
    Poore I / alone, / dreaming, / endure   (8)
        Griefe that / knowes nor/cause, nor/cure.   (7)

Here Campion inverts the first foot in line 2. In line 3, he makes the first foot a spondee and inverts the third. In line 4, by lopping off a syllable, he shifts the rhythm from iambic to trochaic. To appreciate his virtuosity, one has only to rewrite the stanza in regular iambics.

> The lovers teares are sweet, their mover makes them so,
> And proud of wounds the bleeding Souldiers grew.
> But I, alone, in dreams endure
> A Griefe, that knowes nor cause, nor cure.

If asked to name one's favorite poets, it would be meaningless to answer Dante or Shakespeare or Goethe, about whose greatness we are all agreed. One can only name one or two minor poets for whom one feels a particular personal affection, so that, while every competent critic would agree that they are good, one probably rereads them more often and with more delight than most people. In my own case, the two names I would cite are William Barnes and Thomas Campion.

W. H. AUDEN

INTRODUCTION

Our idea of lyric poetry originally comes from a classical Greek distinction between solo songs, sung to the lyre, composed in short stanzas and usually erotic in character; and choral ode, composed in triads of long strophes and of a public, celebratory character when not occurring as part of tragedy or comedy. There were many other classical poetic styles. Elegiac verse was composed in couplets (always unrhymed, as in all classical verse) and was used for satire and epigram, inscription and witty or pointed observation. Iambic verse had a wide range of use, from speeches in plays to drinking songs and love lyrics. Then there was, of course, the continuous hexameter line of epic poetry, and the originally almost startling adaptation of it by Theocritus for his pastoral eclogues.

Latin poets followed and adapted these Greek models, but the actual association of meters with musical forms and styles began to disappear. The Renaissance, extremely self-conscious as it was about classical antiquity, sought to emulate it with a deliberate reunification of music and poetry. England lagged behind the Continent in the development of its music after the death of John Dunstable (1390-1453), one of the most renowned musicians of his day. By the 1580's, however, Italian influences and the invigoration of a native tradition led to a remarkable burst of secular musical activity, and the emergence of a group of composers of the first rank, among them William Byrd, Orlando Gibbons, John Dowland, Thomas Weelkes, Thomas Morley and others. Aside from solo keyboard and lute composition, their main activities were in the field of song. Madrigals were polyphonic settings of poetic texts for several voices, either unaccompanied or, more often, with instruments either doubling the voices or taking their parts.

They were often florid, chromatic and complex, and went to such lengths to avoid stanzaic repetition of different words to the same tune, that they confined themselves to monostrophic poems, like sonnets, or else frequently set two stanzas of the same poem as two different madrigals. Airs, or solo songs, were written for voice and lute (although usually printed with four-part settings included). They were more oriented to a performer-audience situation than the madrigals, whose musico-poetic delights would appeal primarily to one of the singers, hearing the complexities of the setting of the often-repeated words weaving around him. Airs, in addition, were primarily stanzaic: the composer would find a text and set the first stanza, allowing the subsequent ones to be "sung to the same tune," as it were. In the case of frequently banal, metrically smooth poems this "fit" worked very well. In the case of Donne's *Songs and Sonnets*, the tense, wrenched, individualized rhythmic patternings of almost every line made stanzaic settings almost impossible, and with Donne's poems we begin to see texts whose musical settings can best be thought of as the verbal "music" of their own intense speech cadences.

By the 1580's, a variety of poetic conventions had become assimilated to the notion of "liric poem," including "sonnets" in both the strict and loose senses (that is, the familiar fourteen-line iambic pentameter poems as well as any short, Petrarchan love poem), epigrams, pastoral lyrics and so forth. A musician (as Donne puts it in "The Triple Fool"), "his art and voice to show, / Doth set and sing my pain" – and a composer frequently raided miscellanies and anthologies as well as published books and poems in manuscript. Almost any poem might, after publication, show up in a musical setting, sometimes altered for the convenience of the composer.

Although the composers of these songbooks used to be credited, in older and unscholarly anthologies, with the words to their songs, the composer was rarely the poet. Except for an occasional amusing anomaly, like Captain Tobias Hume in his *Poetical Music*, there is only Thomas Campion to maintain, in the English Renaissance, the ancient tradition of the poet-composer. The reputation of another such figure, Chaucer's great contemporary Guillaume de Machaut, has undergone a strange revision in the last fifty years. Before then, philological scholars thought of him as a lyric poet, and it is only modern musicology that has shown how much more interesting his ballades, virelais, and rondeaux were as musical structures than as verse patterns. In short, Machaut is ranked as one of the great composers, and his musical glory has eclipsed his fame as a poet.

Not so with Campion. As a composer he is idiomatic and graceful, seldom tactless but seldom inspired. He worked within the framework of the strophic air always, and never responded to the influence of the new Italian *stilo recitativo* like Alfonso Ferrabosco, nor developed an insistent and personal chromaticism, like John Daniel (brother of the poet Samuel, who refuted Campion's prosodic theories). Neither did he, like John Dowland – who was a virtuoso lutenist of great fame – do anything remarkable with his lute accompaniments; for the most part, they lie easily under the hand, with a minimum of fugal writing and a rather four-square texture.

But as a master of the structure of the stanzaic lyric song text, Campion is unsurpassed in English. He is Sidneyan to the degree that he is preoccupied with elements of what the earlier poet called *architectonike* – the patterning and symmetry of parts of language: lines, grammatical structures, stanzas, and so forth. He is Jonsonian in his response to Latin lyric and elegiac poets, rather than to Sidney's shaping Italian. But he is in a different lyric world from John Donne's, dominated as it is by a rhetorical necessity which overrides repetitive stanzaic principles in the generation of its rhythms and its images. "Strong lines" was the seventeenth-century critical term for metaphysical verse of the Donne tradition. Campion's remain always smooth.

But by no means weak. If his mode was not the skewed, the emphatic and the paradoxical, it remained all the more the delicate, the precise and the epigrammatic. We tend to think of epigram or aphorism primarily in terms of written inscription, rather than chant or song – and indeed, classical tradition assigned epigram to the meter of the elegiac couplet. Yet there were lyrical poems – like the Anacreontea – which Renaissance writers assimilated to such poems as those of the Greek Anthology, and it is not strange to find Campion remarking as follows about the poetic form he made his own:

> *Short Ayres, if they be skilfully framed, and naturally exprest, are like quicke and good Epigrammes in Poesie, many of them shewing as much artifice, and breeding as great difficultie as a large Poeme.*

Let us look at an instance of this. Catullus' famous lyric, *Vivamus, mea Lesbia, atque amemus*, was a background text for many seventeenth-century poems of erotic invitation. Ben Jonson's adaptation of it occurs first as a song in *Volpone* and later in his selection of his favorite poems called *The Forest*. It was set by Ferrabosco, but it remains most powerful as a spoken text:

> Come, my Celia, let us prove,
> While we may, the sports of love;
> Time will not be ours for ever:
> He, at length, our good will sever.
> Spend not then his gifts in vaine.
> Sunnes that set may rise againe:

[18]

But if once we loose this light,
'Tis, with us, perpetuall night.
Why should we deferre our joyes?
Fame and rumour are but toyes.
Cannot we delude the eyes
Of a few poore household spyes?
Or his easier eares beguile
So removed by our wile?
'Tis no sinne, loves fruits to steale,
But the sweete theft to reveale,
To be taken, to be seene,
These have crimes accounted beene.

Campion's reworking of the same Latin original is another matter. Here, he abandons Catullus after the first strophe, and turns the *nox est perpetua una dormienda* from the middle of the poem into a slightly varying refrain, seeing in it unfulfilled lyrical and expository possibilities:

My sweetest Lesbia, let us live and love,
And though the sager sort our deedes reprove,
Let us not way them: heavn's great lamps doe dive
Into their west, and strait againe revive,
But soone as once set is our little light,
Then must we sleepe one ever-during night.

If all would lead their lives in love like mee,
Then bloudie swords and armour should not be,
No drum nor trumpet peaceful sleepes should move,
Unles alarme came from the campe of love:
But fooles do live, and wast their little light,
And seeke with paine their ever-during night.

When timely death my life and fortune ends,
Let not my hearse be vext with mourning friends,
But let all lovers rich in triumph come,

[19]

And with sweet pastimes grace my happie tombe;
And Lesbia close up thou my little light,
And crowne with love my ever-during night.

This is the *carpe diem* theme further humanized and matured by an awareness of the *memento mori* aspect of it: the vision of dying in love, and for it, and having love made on one's tomb, is a sweeter one than we find in Jonson's "let us do it while we can," or, later on in the century, the sardonic energy of Marvell's "To His Coy Mistress."

In this poem, too, it is as if the stanzaic limitations were a source of creative energy for Campion, rather than a restraint. Throughout the corpus of songs we can see this energy at work – whether in a hymn, like the lovely "Never Weather-Beaten Saile," a magic spell like "Thrice Toss These Oaken Ashes in the Aire" or a half-parodic comment on the burning brands of Eros in "Fire, Fire, Fire Fire." The development of a theme and its disposition throughout the successive strophes is always his forte. Take, for example, the justly famous "Cherry-Ripe," which takes off from the most common of street cries, the *"Cherry ripe ripe ripe!"* of the cherry vendor, sung, as we know from other early seventeenth-century evidence, through an ascending third:

Cher-ry ripe, ripe, ripe!

Whether the sung phrase as Campion recalled it suggested the garden conceit (Herrick wrote a little poem starting with the same repeated words of the street cry), or whether it crept in as the basic image was unfolding, the result was a wonderful transformation of a whole series of commonplaces:

There is a Garden in her face,
Where Roses and white Lillies grow;

[20]

A heav'nly paradice is that place,
Wherein all pleasant fruits do flow.
 There Cherries grow, which none may buy
 Till Cherry ripe themselves doe cry.

Those Cherries fairly doe enclose
Of Orient Pearle a double row;
 Which when her lovely laughter showes,
They look like Rose-buds fill'd with snow.
 Yet them nor Peere nor Prince can buy,
 Till Cherry ripe themselves doe cry.

 Her Eyes like Angels watch them still;
Her Browes like bended bowes doe stand,
 Threatning with piercing frownes to kill
All that attempt with eye or hand
 Those sacred Cherries to come nigh,
 Till Cherry ripe themselves doe cry.

In the first strophe, we may let the significance of "heav'nly paradice" go by, thinking it a mere hyperbole as conventional as the roses and lilies of the blazon, or Petrarchan catalogue of delights – the red of feeling and the white of purity which combine in the "carnation" or flesh tone in emblematic color language (the Elizabethans seem not to have had our term "pink"). We may even miss an echo, in the use of "flow" for "abound," of the Biblical "flowing with milk and honey," seeing only the image extending through the refrain: the lady's lips which alone are able to say "yes" for her, are like wares that advertise themselves. But then, in the second stanza, rosebuds filled with snow and pearls in a garden both emphasize the neglected "paradice." Here are all seasons at once, and the natural and artificial are confounded: we are in the neighborhood of the earthly paradises of Spenser and his followers. The final stanza, in which the cherries become "sacred" and assimilated mythologically to the golden apples of the Hesperides, shows us the garden as being angelically protected (the old Petrarchan cliché about frowning eyebrows being like drawn bows is redeemed in this new association). The courtly compliment now turns out to be central moral vision: the only *paradiso terrestre* or Earthly Paradise is to be found in beautiful sexual attainment, in the plucking of cherries that are no forbidden apples, and just for that reason, such attainment isn't always easy. Campion's stanzaic development has served the imaginative purpose of taking seriously what might be, in a weaker song by a less serious and joyful singer, a bit of lyrical rhetoric.

In his musical setting of the poem in his *Fourth Booke of Ayres*, Campion cannot help working the melodic phrase of the street cry itself into his refrain. Imitative and referential bits of musical setting like this abound in later Elizabethan and Jacobean musical practice, and Campion employs them occasionally with a certain amount of delight. Thus

> When to her lute Corinna sings,
> Her voice revives the leaden stringes,
> And doth in highest noates appeare,
> As any challeng'd echo cleere;
> But when she doth of sorrow speake,
> Ev'n from my hart the strings do breake.

– and there is an expressive downward turn of the vocal line underlined by a chordal sweep on the lute to suggest the breaking strings. The second strophe, incidentally, moralizes the anecdote in conventional fashion, applying it to the poet's own feelings, and concluding with a familiar Elizabethan invocation of "heartstrings" (the term's literary popularity resulted from a Latin pun on *cor, cordis*: "heart" and *chorda*: "string"). But the musical setting of the first stanza must remain effective for the second, and the heart-strings must "break" as well, the figurative heartbreak echoing the damage to the instrument:

> And as her lute doth live or die,
> Led by her passion, so must I,
> For when of pleasure she doth sing,
> My thoughts enjoy a sodaine spring,
> But if she doth of sorrow speake,
> Ev'n from my hart the strings doe breake.

Many of Campion's songs concern, or involve imagery about, music and its effects as celebrated in mythology: "Follow Your Saint," "To Musicke Bent Is My Retyred Minde," "Tune Thy Musicke to Thy Hart," "To His Sweet Lute Apollo Sung the Motions of the Spheares," for example; and much in the masques and court entertainments celebrate music and thereby, given Campion's personal and learned neoclassical association of the two, of poetry as well. Even in his metrical version of the 137th Psalm ("By the waters of Babylon"), Campion pays special attention to the musical possibilities of "We hanged our harps upon the willows in the midst thereof," and gives us

> Aloft the trees, that sprung up there,
> Our silent Harps wee pensive hung"

playing deliciously on the etymological connection of "pensive" and the Latin *pendere*: "to hang."

Even, too, the metrical example, "Rose-cheekt Lawra" – surely the most successful "exercise," qua poem, in our tradition – affirms a platonistic correspondence between actual and ideal, based on an avowed relation between heavenly harmony and human music:

> Rose-cheekt *Lawra*, come,
> Sing thou smoothly with thy beawties

[23]

Silent musick, either other
Sweetely gracing.

Lovely formes do flowe
From concent divinely framed;
Heav'n is musick, and thy beawties
Birth is heavenly . . .

This beautiful little poem occurs in Campion's cranky *Observations on the Art of English Poesie,* a treatise on poetic meter whose attack on rhyme, and championing of classical prosody over native English verse structure, seems pointless to us today. The Elizabethans are, after all, our poetic Greek and Latin poets – the English past is our linguistic and imaginative antiquity; the iambic pentameter is our classical verse. But at the end of the sixteenth century, the desire to legitimize a national English literature by giving it good classical credentials still led some poets and critics to espouse a literal adoption of the quantitative meters of Greek and Latin poetry. This cannot be done in English, with its prominent word stress, save by assigning Latin vowel lengths to the written English, and simply patterning what amounts to a typographical code which cannot be heard as verse. Thus, a translator of a passage from Ovid in a songbook of William Byrd starts out with one of those pseudo-quantitative lines which reads

Constant Penelope sends to thee, careless Ulysses

– and which *sounds* like a five-beat dactylic line in English rhythms: *Bumpity, Bumpity, Bumpity, Bumpity Bum-Bum.* The poet, however, by a dark process of giving values to letters in syllables rather than to sounds, was writing

Constant Penelope sends to thee, careless Ulysses

– or at least this is what Byrd assumed he meant, from the

note values he gave it in setting. This may make sense to the sufficiently learned eye, perhaps, but to no ear.

Campion was a loyal neoclassical ideologue in the controversies about metrics. In his "Preface to the Reader" in his 1601 *Book of Ayres*, he speaks slightingly of the normal English accentual-syllabic verse in which all his airs but one are composed; they are, he says "after the fascion of the time, eare-pleasing rimes without Arte." Fortunately, he never rode his hobby-horse over the living bodies of his songs. Even in his treatise, he adapts the prevailing sort of quantitative written coding of English so that his "long" syllables are always the ones bearing the stress-accent of the word. "Rose-cheekt Lawra" is therefore merely an unrhymed English trochaic poem, perfectly plain to the ear. Campion's one song in classical meters which concludes his first book of airs, "Come let us sound with melody the praises," is set for voice and lute, with note values corresponding to syllable length, in a fashion followed in Byrd's setting mentioned above, perhaps derived from a French tradition. But his unerring sense of iambic rhythm and its controlled rhetorical possibilities prevailed over his schematic beliefs.

That rhythmic sense is everywhere parallelled by other modes of stylistic tactfulness – of degree and depth of allusion to classical models and themes; of length to which a conceit is drawn out; of the subjugation of wit and literary ambition to the limits of the song form he could make his own. His conventional Petrarchan vocabulary and imagery of love are never used mechanically, and his wit never allows empty gesture to depose verbal act. I can think of no better example of Campion's lyrical good humor than his ability to undercut even his own conventional delicacy with an equally graceful anti-Petrarchan move. First, from the 1601 book:

> Mistris, since you so much desire
> To know the place of Cupid's fire,

In your faire shrine that flame doth rest,
Yet never harbourd in your brest,
It bides not in your lips so sweete,
Nor where the rose and lillies meete
But a little higher, but a little higher;
There, there, O there lies Cupids fire.

Even in those starrie piercing eyes,
There Cupids sacred fire lyes.
Those eyes I strive not to enjoy,
For they have power to destroy.
Nor woe I for a smile, or kisse,
So meanely triumphs not my blisse,
But a little higher, but a little higher,
I climbe to crowne my chaste desire.

The lady's eyes, the source of higher love than is her mouth, are here celebrated in the language of the sonneteers: the air of sanctity, the rejection of "meane" triumphs of mere passion, etc., are all familiar. But here are Campion's second thoughts, from the *Fourth Booke of Ayres*:

Beauty, since you so much desire
To know the place of *Cupids* fire,
About you somewhere doth it rest,
Yet never harbour'd in your brest,
Nor gout-like in your heele or toe;
What foole would seeke Loves flame so low?
But a little higher, but a little higher,
There, there, ô there lyes *Cupids* fire.

Thinke not, when *Cupid* most you scorne,
Men judge that you of Ice were borne;
For though you cast love at your heele,
His fury yet sometime you feele:
And where-abouts if you would know,

[26]

I tell you still not in your toe:
But a little higher, but a little higher,
There, there, ô there lyes *Cupids* fire.

This is a satiric reduction, a literal *lowering*: here love starts,
as in Donne's "Love's Progresse," from below, so that it may
find its home in sex, at the body's center. Campion's setting
for the second song is a bit more chromatic in melodic line
than the first, and the lute part points up the repeatedly
ascending "but a little higher" with contrapuntal nudging.
These two songs, idealizing and faintly bawdy, are in a
way two sides of the same Elizabethan coin. To have been
unable to toss it and cope with head or tail with equal
ease would have evidenced a want of invention and a false
decorum from which Campion, for all the limitations of
his poetic chamber music, can never be said to suffer.

JOHN HOLLANDER

[27]

SONGS

From
Songs appended to Sidney's
Astrophel and Stella

CANTO SECUNDO

What faire pompe have I spide of glittering Ladies;
With locks sparckled abroad, and rosie Coronet
On their yvorie browes, trackt to the daintie thies
With roabs like *Amazons*, blew as Violet,
With gold Aglets adornd, some in a changeable
Pale, with spangs wavering, taught to be moveable.

Then those Knights that a farre off with dolorous viewing
Cast their eyes hetherward: loe, in an agonie,
All unbrac'd, crie aloud, their heavie state ruing:
Moyst cheekes with blubbering, painted as *Ebonie*
Blacke; their feltred haire torne with wrathfull hand:
And whiles astonied, starke in a maze they stand.

But hearke, what merry sound! what sodaine harmonie!
Looke, looke neere the grove where the Ladies doe tread
With their knights the measures waide by the melodie!
Wantons, whose travesing make men enamoured!
Now they faine an honor, now by the slender wast
He must lift hir aloft, and seale a kisse in hast.

Streight downe under a shadow for wearines they lie
With pleasant daliance, hand knit with arme in arme;
Now close, now set aloof, they gaze with an equall eie,
Changing kisses alike; streight with a false alarme,
Mocking kisses alike, powt with a lovely lip.
Thus drownd with jollities, their merry daies doe slip.

But stay! now I discerne they goe on a Pilgrimage
Toward Loves holy land, faire *Paphos* or *Cyprus*.
Such devotion is meete for a blithesome age;
With sweet youth it agrees well to be amorous.
Let olde angrie fathers lurke in an Hermitage:
Come, weele associate this jollie Pilgrimage!

From

A Book of Ayres

PART ONE

I

My sweetest Lesbia, let us live and love,
And, though the sager sort our deedes reprove,
Let us not way them: heav'ns great lampes doe dive
Into their west, and strait againe revive,
But, soone as once set is our little light,
Then must we sleepe one ever-during night.

If all would lead their lives in love like mee,
Then bloudie swords and armour should not be,
No drum nor trumpet peaceful sleepes should move,
Unles alar'me came from the campe of love:
But fooles do live, and wast their little light,
And seeke with paine their ever-during night.

When timely death my life and fortune ends,
Let not my hearse be vext with mourning friends,
But let all lovers, rich in triumph, come,
And with sweet pastimes grace my happie tombe;
And, Lesbia, close up thou my little light,
And crowne with love my ever-during night.

My sweet - est Les — — bia, let us live and love,

And, though the sa — ger sort our deedes re - - prove,

Let us not way them: heav'ns great lampes doe

dive In - to their west, and strait a - gaine re - vive,

But, soone as once set is our lit - tle light, Then must we sleepe one e - ver-dur-ing night, e - - ver - dur - ing night.

III

I care not for these Ladies
That must be woode and praide,
Give me kind Amarillis
The wanton countrey maide;
Nature art disdaineth,
Her beautie is her owne;
    Her when we court and kisse,
    She cries, forsooth, let go:
    But when we come where comfort is,
    She never will say no.

If I love Amarillis,
She gives me fruit and flowers,
But if we love these Ladies,
We must give golden showers;
Give them gold that sell love,
Give me the Nutbrowne lasse,
    Who when we court and kisse,
    She cries, forsooth, let go:
    But when we come where comfort is,
    She never will say no.

These Ladies must have pillowes,
And beds by strangers wrought,
Give me a Bower of willowes,
Of mosse and leaves unbought,
And fresh Amarillis,
With milke and honie fed,
    Who when we court and kisse,
    She cries, forsooth, let go:
    But when we come where comfort is,
    She never will say no.

I care not for these La - dies That must be woode and praide,
Give me kind A - ma - ril - lis The wan - ton coun - trey maide;

Na - ture art dis - dain - eth, Her beau - tie is her owne;

Her when we_ court and kisse, She cries, for - sooth, let go:

But when we come where com - fort is, she_ ne - ver_ will say no.

[41]

IIII

Followe thy faire sunne, unhappy shaddowe:
Though thou be blacke as night,
And she made all of light,
Yet follow thy faire sunne, unhappie shaddowe.

Follow her whose light thy light depriveth:
Though here thou liv'st disgrac't,
And she in heaven is plac't,
Yet follow her whose light the world reviveth.

Follow those pure beames whose beautie burneth,
That so have scorched thee,
As thou still blacke must bee,
Til her kind beames thy black to brightnes turneth.

Follow her while yet her glorie shineth:
There comes a luckles night,
That will dim all her light;
And this the black unhappie shade devineth.

Follow still since so thy fates ordained:
The Sunne must have his shade,
Till both at once doe fade,
The Sun still prov'd, the shadow still disdained.

Fol - lowe thy faire sunne, un - hap - py shad-dowe:

Though thou, though thou be blacke as night, And she made all of light, Yet fol - low thy faire sunne, un - hap — pie— shad — — dowe.

X

Follow your Saint, follow with accents sweet,
Haste you, sad noates, fall at her flying feete;
There, wrapt in cloud of sorrowe, pitie move,
And tell the ravisher of my soule I perish for her love.
But if she scorns my never-ceasing paine,
Then burst with sighing in her sight, and nere returne
                                          againe.

All that I song still to her praise did tend,
Still she was first, still she my songs did end.
Yet she my love and Musicke both doeth flie,
The Musicke that her Eccho is, and beauties simpathie;
Then let my Noates pursue her scornefull flight:
It shall suffice that they were breath'd, and dyed, for her
                                          delight.

Fol - low your Saint, fol - low with ac - cents sweet,
Haste you, sad noates, fall at her fly - ing feete;

There, wrapt in cloud of sor - rowe, pi - tie move, And tell the
But if she scorns my ne - ver - ceas - ing paine, Then burst with

rav - ish - er of my soule I per - ish for her love.
sigh - ing in her sight, and nere re - turne a - gaine.

XI

Faire, if you expect admiring,
Sweet, if you provoke desiring,
Grace deere love with kinde requiting.
Fond, but if thy sight be blindnes,
False, if thou affect unkindnes,
Flie both love and loves delighting.
Then when hope is lost and love is scorned,
Ile bury my desires, and quench the fires that ever yet in
          vaine have burned.

Fates, if you rule lovers fortune,
Stars, if men your powers importune,
Yield reliefe by your relenting.
Time, if sorrow be not endles,
Hope made vaine, and pittie friendles,
Helpe to ease my long lamenting.
But if griefes remaine still unredressed,
I'le flie to her againe, and sue for pitie to renue my hopes
          distressed.

XVII

Your faire lookes enflame my desire:
  Quench it againe with love.
Stay, O strive not still to retire,
  Doe not inhumane prove.
If love may perswade,
  Loves pleasures, deere, denie not;
Here is a silent grovie shade:
  O tarrie then, and flie not.

Have I seaz'd my heavenly delight
  In this unhaunted grove?
Time shall now her furie requite
  With the revenge of love.
Then come, sweetest, come,
  My lips with kisses gracing:
Heere let us harbour all alone,
  Die, die in sweete embracing.

Will you now so timely depart,
  And not returne againe?
Your sight lends such life to my hart
  That to depart is paine.
Feare yeelds no delay,
  Securenes helpeth pleasure:
Then, till the time gives safer stay,
  O farewell, my lives treasure!

XIX

Harke, al you ladies that do sleep:
   the fayry queen Proserpina
Bids you awake and pitie them that weep;
  you may doe in the darke
What the day doth forbid:
   feare not the dogs that barke,
        Night will have all hid.

But if you let your lovers mone,
   the Fairie Queene Proserpina
Will send abroad her Fairies ev'rie one,
   that shall pinch blacke and blew
Your white hands, and faire armes,
   that did not kindly rue
        Your Paramours harmes.

In Myrtle Arbours on the downes,
   the Fairie Queene Proserpina,
This night by moone-shine leading merrie rounds,
   holds a watch with sweet love;
Downe the dale, up the hill,
   no plaints or groanes may move
        Their holy vigill.

All you that will hold watch with love,
   the Fairie Queene Proserpina
Will make you fairer then Diones dove;
   Roses red, Lillies white,
And the cleare damaske hue,
   shall on your cheekes alight:
        Love will adorne you.

All you that love, or lov'd before,
   the Fairie Queene Proserpina
Bids you encrease that loving humour more:
   they that yet have not fed
On delight amorous,
   she vowes that they shall lead
        Apes in Avernus.

XX

When thou must home to shades of under ground,
And there ariv'd, a newe admired guest,
The beauteous spirits do ingirt thee round,
White Iope, blith Hellen, and the rest,
To heare the stories of thy finisht love,
From that smoothe toong whose musicke hell can move:

Then wilt thou speake of banqueting delights,
Of masks and revels which sweete youth did make,
Of Turnies and great challenges of knights,
And all these triumphes for thy beauties sake:
When thou hast told these honours done to thee,
Then tell, O tell, how thou didst murther me.

From
Two Bookes of Ayres

I

Author of light, revive my dying spright,
Redeeme it from the snares of all-confounding night.
      Lord, light me to thy blessed way:
For, blinde with worldly vaine desires, I wander as a stray.
      Sunne and Moone, Starres and underlights I see,
But all their glorious beames are mists and darknes, being
                            compar'd to thee.

Fountaine of health, my soules deepe wounds recure,
Sweet showres of pitty raine, wash my uncleannesse pure.
      One drop of thy desired grace
The faint and fading hart can raise, and in joyes bosome
                               place.
      Sinne and Death, Hell and tempting Fiends may rage;
But God his owne will guard, and their sharp paines and
                        griefe in time asswage.

IIII

Out of my soules deapth to thee my cryes have sounded:
Let thine eares my plaints receive, on just feare grounded.
Lord, should'st thou weigh our faults, who's not
                                                 confounded?

But with grace thou censur'st thine when they have erred,
Therefore shall thy blessed name be lov'd and feared:
Ev'n to thy throne my thoughts and eyes are reared.

Thee alone my hopes attend, on thee relying;
In thy sacred word I'le trust, to thee fast flying,
Long ere the Watch shall breake, the morne descrying.

In the mercies of our God who live secured,
May of full redemption rest in him assured;
Their sinne-sicke soules by him shall be recured.

VII

To Musicke bent is my retyred minde,
And faine would I some song of pleasure sing:
But in vaine joyes no comfort now I finde:
From heav'nly thoughts all true delight doth spring.
Thy power, O God, thy mercies to record
Will sweeten ev'ry note, and ev'ry word.

All earthly pompe or beauty to expresse,
Is but to carve in snow, on waves to write.
Celestiall things, though men conceive them lesse,
Yet fullest are they in themselves of light:
Such beames they yeeld as know no meanes to dye:
Such heate they cast as lifts the Spirit high.

To Mus-icke bent is my re-tyr-ed minde,
But in vaine joyes no com-fort now I finde:

faine would I some song of pleas-ure sing:
heav'n-ly thoughts all true de-light doth spring.

Thy power, O God, thy mer-cies to re-cord Will

sweet-en ev-'ry note, and ev-'ry word.

[57]

XI

Never weather-beaten Saile more willing bent to shore,
Never tyred Pilgrims limbs affected slumber more,
Then my weary spright now longs to flye out of my
                                        troubled brest.
  O come quickly, sweetest Lord, and take my soule to rest,

Ever-blooming are the joyes of Heav'ns high paradice,
Cold age deafes not there our eares, nor vapour dims
                                        our eyes;
Glory there the Sun outshines, whose beames the blessed
                                        onely see:
  O come quickly, glorious Lord, and raise my spright
                                        to thee.

Ne - ver wea - ther - bea - ten Saile more wil - ling bent to shore,
Ne - ver ty - red Pil - grims limbs af - fe - cted slum - ber more,

Then my wea - ry spright now longs to flye out of my

trou - bled brest. O come quick - ly, O come quick - ly,

O come quickly, sweet - est Lord, and take my soule to rest.

XVII

Come, chearfull day, part of my life, to mee:
For, while thou view'st me with thy fading light,
Part of my life doth still depart with thee,
And I still onward haste to my last night.
    Times fatal wings doe ever forward flye,
    Soe ev'ry day we live, a day wee dye.

But, O yee nights ordain'd for barren rest,
How are my dayes depriv'd of life in you,
When heavy sleepe my soule hath dispossest,
By fayned death life sweetly to renew!
    Part of my life, in that, you life denye:
    So ev'ry day we live, a day wee dye.

XVIII

Seeke the Lord, and in his wayes persever:
  O faint not, but as Eagles flye,
  For his steepe hill is high;
Then, striving, gaine the top, and triumph ever.

When with glory there thy browes are crowned,
  New joyes so shall abound in thee,
  Such sights thy soule shall see,
That wordly thoughts shall by their beames be drowned.

Farewell, World, thou masse of meere confusion,
  False light with many shadowes dimm'd,
  Old Witch with new foyles trimm'd,
Thou deadly sleepe of soule, and charm'd illusion.

I the King will seeke of Kings adored,
  Spring of light, tree of grace and blisse,
  Whose fruit so sov'raigne is
That all who taste it are from death restored.

XX

Jacke and *Jone*, they thinke no ill,
But loving live, and merry still;
Doe their weeke dayes worke, and pray
Devotely on the holy day;
Skip and trip it on the greene,
And help to chuse the Summer Queene;
Lash out, at a Country Feast,
Their silver penny with the best.

Well can they judge of nappy Ale,
And tell at large a Winter tale;
Climbe up to the Apple loft,
And turne the Crabs till they be soft.
Tib is all the fathers joy,
And little *Tom* the mothers boy.
All their pleasure is content;
And care, to pay their yearely rent.

Jone can call by name her Cowes,
And decke her windowes with greene boughs;
Shee can wreathes and tuttyes make,
And trimme with plums a Bridall Cake.
Jacke knowes what brings gaine or losse,
And his long Flaile can stoutly tosse;
Make the hedge, which others breake,
And ever thinkes what he doth speake.

Now, you Courtly Dames and Knights,
That study onely strange delights,
Though you scorne the home-spun gray,
And revell in your rich array;

Though your tongues dissemble deepe,
And can your heads from danger keepe;
Yet, for all your pompe and traine,
Securer lives the silly Swaine.

XXI

All lookes be pale, harts cold as stone.
For *Hally* now is dead, and gone,
    Hally, in whose sight,
      Most sweet sight,
    All the earth late tooke delight.
  Ev'ry eye, weepe with mee,
  Joyes drown'd in teares must be.

His Iv'ry skin, his comely hayre,
His Rosie cheekes, so cleare and faire,
    Eyes that once did grace
      His bright face,
    Now in him all want their place.
  Eyes and hearts, weepe with mee,
  For who so kinde as hee?

His youth was like an *Aprill* flowre,
Adorn'd with beauty, love, and powre;
    Glory strow'd his way,
      Whose wreaths gay
    Now are all turn'd to decay.
  Then againe weepe with mee,
  None feele more cause then wee.

No more may his wisht sight returne,
His golden Lampe no more can burne;
    Quencht is all his flame,
      His hop't fame
    Now hath left him nought but name.
  For him all weepe with mee,
  Since more him none shall see.

All lookes be pale, harts cold as stone. For Hal-ly now is dead, and

gone, Hal - ly, in whose sight, Most sweet sight, All the earth late tooke de -

light. Ev-'ry eye, weepe with mee, weepe with mee,

weepe with mee, Joyes drown'd in teares must be, Joyes drown'd in teares must be.

VI

Faine would I my love disclose,
Aske what honour might denye;
But both love and her I lose,
From my motion if shee flye.
Worse then paine is feare to mee:
Then hold in fancy, though it burne;
If not happy, safe Ile be,
And to my clostred cares returne.

Yet, o yet, in vaine I strive
To represse my school'd desire;
More and more the flames revive,
I consume in mine owne fire.
She would pitty, might shee know
The harmes that I for her endure:
Speake then, and get comfort so:
A wound long hid growes past recure.

Wise shee is, and needs must know
All th' attempts that beauty moves:
Fayre she is, and honour'd so
That she, sure, hath tryed some loves.
If with love I tempt her then,
'Tis but her due to be desir'd:
What would women thinke of men,
If their deserts were not admir'd?

Women, courted, have the hand
To discard what they distaste:
But those Dames whom none demand
Want oft what their wils imbrac't.
Could their firmnesse iron excell,
As they are faire, they should be sought:
When true theeves use falsehood well,
As they are wise, they will be caught.

XII

The peacefull westerne winde
The winter stormes hath tam'd,
And nature in each kinde
The kinde heat hath inflam'd.
The forward buds so sweetly breathe
　　Out of their earthy bowers,
That heav'n, which viewes their pompe beneath,
　　Would faine be deckt with flowers.

　　See how the morning smiles
　　On her bright easterne hill,
　　And with soft steps beguiles
　　Them that lie slumbring still.
The musicke-loving birds are come
　　From cliffes and rockes unknowne,
To see the trees and briers blome
　　That late were over-flowne.

　　What Saturne did destroy,
　　Loves Queene revives againe;
　　And now her naked boy
　　Doth in the fields remaine:
Where he such pleasing change doth view
　　In ev'ry living thing,
As if the world were borne anew
　　To gratifie the Spring.

　　If all things life present,
　　Why die my comforts then?
　　Why suffers my content?
　　Am I the worst of men?

O beautie, be not thou accus'd
    Too justly in this case:
Unkindly if true love be us'd,
    'Twill yeeld thee little grace.

XVI

Though your strangenesse frets my hart,
Yet may not I complaine:
You perswade me, 'tis but Art,
That secret love must faine.
If another you affect,
'Tis but a shew t' avoid suspect.
Is this faire excusing? O no, all is abusing.

Your wisht sight if I desire,
Suspitions you pretend;
Causelesse you your selfe retire,
While I in vaine attend.
This a Lover whets, you say,
Still made more eager by delay.
Is this faire excusing? O no, all is abusing.

When another holds your hand,
You sweare I hold your hart:
When my Rivals close doe stand
And I sit farre apart,
I am neerer yet then they,
Hid in your bosome, as you say.
Is this faire excusing? O no, all is abusing.

Would my Rival then I were,
Some els your secret friend:
So much lesser should I feare,
And not so much attend.
They enjoy you, ev'ry one,
Yet I must seeme your friend alone.
Is this faire excusing? O no, all is abusing.

Though your strange-nesse frets my hart, Yet may not I com-plaine:
You per-swade me, 'tis but Art, That se-cret love must faine.

If a-no-ther you af-fect, 'Tis but a shew t'a-void su-

spect. Is this faire ex-cu-sing? O no, all is a-bus-ing.

XVIII

Come, you pretty false-ey'd wanton,
 Leave your crafty smiling:
Thinke you to escape me now
 With slipp'ry words beguiling?
No; you mock't me th' other day,
 When you got loose, you fled away;
But, since I have caught you now,
 Ile clip your wings for flying:
Smothring kisses fast Ile heape,
 And keepe you so from crying.

Sooner may you count the starres,
 And number hayle downe pouring,
Tell the Osiers of the *Temmes*,
 Or *Goodwins* Sands devouring,
Then the thicke-showr'd kisses here
 Which now thy tyred lips must beare.
Such a harvest never was,
 So rich and full of pleasure,
But 'tis spent as soone as reapt,
 So trustlesse is loves treasure.

Would it were dumb midnight now,
 When all the world lyes sleeping:
Would this place some Desert were,
 Which no man hath in keeping.
My desires should then be safe,
 And when you cry'd then would I laugh;
But if ought might breed offence,
 Love onely should be blamed:
I would live your servant still,
 And you my Saint unnamed.

Come, you pret - ty false-ey'd wan - ton, Leave your craf - ty smil - ing:
Thinke you to es-cape me now With slip-p'ry words be - guil - ing?

No; you mock't me th'o-ther day, When you got loose, you fled a - way;

But, since I have caught you now, Ile clip your wings for fly - ing:
Smoth-ring kiss - es fast Ile heape, And keepe you so from cry - ing.

XIX

A secret love or two, I must confesse,
 I kindly welcome for change in close playing:
Yet my deare husband I love ne'erthelesse,
 His desires, whole or halfe, quickly allaying,
At all times ready to offer redresse.
 His owne he never wants, but hath it duely,
 Yet twits me, I keepe not touch with him truly.

The more a spring is drawne, the more it flowes;
 No Lampe lesse light retaines by lighting others:
Is hee a looser his losse that ne're knowes?
 Or is he wealthy that wast treasure smothers?
My churle vowes no man shall sent his sweet Rose:
 His owne enough and more I give him duely,
 Yet still he twits mee, I keepe not touch truly.

Wise Archers beare more then one shaft to field,
 The Venturer loads not with one ware his shipping:
Should Warriers learne but one weapon to weilde?
 Or thrive faire plants ere the worse for the slipping?
One dish cloyes, many fresh appetite yeeld:
 Mine owne Ile use, and his he shall have duely,
 Judge then what debter can keepe touch more truly.

From
The Third and Fourth Booke of Ayres

III

Were my hart as some mens are, thy errours would not
                                                    move me:
But thy faults I curious finde, and speake because I love
                                                      thee;
Patience is a thing divine and farre, I grant, above mee.

Foes sometimes befriend us more, our blacker deedes
                                              objecting,
Then th' obsequious bosome guest, with false respect
                                             affecting:
Friendship is the glasse of Truth, our hidden staines
                                            detecting.

While I use of eyes enjoy, and inward light of reason,
Thy observer will I be, and censor, but in season:
Hidden mischiefe to conceale in State and Love is treason.

V

So tyr'd are all my thoughts, that sence and spirits faile;
Mourning I pine, and know not what I ayle.
O what can yeeld ease to a minde,
    Joy in nothing that can finde?

How are my powres fore-spoke? what strange distaste
                                          is this?
Hence, cruell hate of that which sweetest is:
Come, come delight, make my dull braine
    Feele once heate of joy againe.

The lovers teares are sweet, their mover makes them so;
Proud of a wound the bleeding Souldiers grow:
Poore I alone, dreaming, endure
    Griefe that knowes nor cause, nor cure.

And whence can all this grow? even from an idle minde,
That no delight in any good can finde.
Action alone makes the soule blest:
    Vertue dyes with too much rest.

VII

Kinde are her answeres,
    But her performance keeps no day,
Breaks time, as dancers
    From their own Musicke when they stray:
    All her free favors
And smooth words wing my hopes in vaine.
O did ever voice so sweet but only fain?
    Can true love yeeld such delay,
    Converting joy to pain?

Lost is our freedome
    When we submit to women so:
Why doe wee neede them,
    When in their best they worke our woe?
    There is no wisedome
Can alter ends by Fate prefixt:
O why is the good of man with evill mixt?
    Never were dayes yet cal'd two,
    But one night went betwixt.

X

Breake now my heart and dye! Oh no, she may relent.
Let my despaire prevayle! Oh stay, hope is not spent.
Should she now fixe one smile on thee, where were
                                                    despaire?
    The losse is but easie which smiles can repayre.
    A stranger would please thee, if she were as fayre.

Her must I love or none, so sweet none breathes as shee;
The more is my despayre, alas, shee loves not mee:
But cannot time make way for love through ribs of steele?
    The Grecian, inchanted all parts but the heele,
    At last a shaft daunted, which his hart did feele.

XII

Now winter nights enlarge
  The number of their houres,
And clouds their stormes discharge
  Upon the ayrie towres;
Let now the chimneys blaze
  And cups o'erflow with wine,
Let well-tun'd words amaze
  With harmonie divine.
Now yellow waxen lights
  Shall waite on hunny Love,
While youthfull Revels, Masks, and Courtly sights,
  Sleepes leaden spels remove.

This time doth well dispence
  With lovers long discourse;
Much speech hath some defence,
  Though beauty no remorse.
All doe not all things well:
  Some measures comely tread,
Some knotted Ridles tell,
  Some Poems smoothly read.
The Summer hath his joyes,
  And Winter his delights;
Though Love and all his pleasures are but toyes,
  They shorten tedious nights.

Now win - ter nights en - large The num-ber of their houres, And
Let now the chim-neys blaze And cups o'er - flow with wine, Let

clouds their stormes dis - charge Up - on the ayr - ie towres.
well - tun'd words a - maze With har - mo - nie di - vine.

Now yel - low wax - en lights Shall waite on hun-ny Love, While

youth-full Rev - els, Masks, and Court-ly sights, Sleepes lead - en spels re - move.

[83]

XIII

Awake, thou spring of speaking grace, mute rest becomes
not thee;
The fayrest women, while they sleepe, and Pictures equall
bee.
O come and dwell in loves discourses,
Old renuing, new creating.
The words which thy rich tongue discourses
Are not of the common rating.

Thy voyce is as an Eccho cleare which Musicke doth beget,
Thy speech is as an Oracle which none can counterfeit:
For thou alone, without offending,
Hast obtain'd power of enchanting;
And I could heare thee without ending,
Other comfort never wanting.

Some little reason brutish lives with humane glory share;
But language is our proper grace, from which they sever'd
are.
As brutes in reason man surpasses,
Men in speech excell each other:
If speech be then the best of graces,
Doe it not in slumber smother.

XVI

If thou longst so much to learne (sweet boy) what 'tis to
love,
Doe but fixe thy thought on mee, and thou shalt quickly
prove.
　　Little sute, at first, shal win
　　　Way to thy abasht desire,
　　But then will I hedge thee in,
　　　Salamander-like, with fire.

With thee dance I will, and sing, and thy fond dalliance
beare;
Wee the grovy hils will climbe, and play the wantons there;
　　Other whiles wee'le gather flowres,
　　　Lying dalying on the grasse,
　　And thus our delightfull howres
　　　Full of waking dreames shall passe.

When thy joyes were thus at height, my love should turne
from thee;
Old acquaintance then should grow as strange as strange
might be;
　　Twenty rivals thou should'st finde
　　　Breaking all their hearts for mee,
　　When to all Ile prove more kinde
　　　And more forward then to thee.

Thus thy silly youth, enrag'd, would soone my love defie;
But, alas, poore soule, too late: clipt wings can never flye.
　　Those sweet houres which wee had past,
　　　Cal'd to minde, thy heart would burne;
　　And, could'st thou flye ne'er so fast,
　　　They would make thee straight returne.

XVII

Shall I come, sweet Love, to thee,
    When the ev'ning beames are set?
Shall I not excluded be?
        Will you finde no fained lett?
            Let me not, for pitty, more,
                Tell the long houres at your dore.

Who can tell what theefe or foe,
    In the covert of the night,
For his prey, will worke my woe,
        Or through wicked foule despight:
            So may I dye unredrest,
                Ere my long love be possest.

But, to let such dangers passe,
    Which a lovers thoughts disdaine,
'Tis enough in such a place
        To attend loves joyes in vaine.
            Doe not mocke me in thy bed,
                While these cold nights freeze me dead.

Shall I come, sweet Love, to thee, When the ev'-ning beames are
set? Shall I not ex-clud-ed be? Will you finde no fain-ed
lett? Let me not, for pit - ty, more, Tell the long, long
houres, tell the long houres at your dore. Let me dore.

XX

Fire, fire, fire, fire!
Loe here I burne in such desire
That all the teares that I can straine
Out of mine idle empty braine
Cannot allay my scorching paine.
　　Come *Trent*, and *Humber*, and fayre *Thames*,
　　Dread Ocean, haste with all thy streames:
　　And, if you cannot quench my fire,
　　O drowne both mee and my desire.

　　Fire, fire, fire, fire!
There is no hell to my desire:
See, all the Rivers backward flye,
And th' Ocean doth his waves deny,
For feare my heate should drinke them dry.
　　Come, heav'nly showres, then, pouring downe;
　　Come, you that once the world did drowne:
　　Some then you spar'd, but now save all,
　　That else must burne, and with mee fall.

Fire,— fire, fire,— fire! Loe here I burne, I
burne in such de - sire, That all the teares that
I can straine Out of mine i - dle emp - ty
braine Can - not al - lay my scorch - ing paine.

[89]

Come Trent, and Hum - ber, and fayre Thames, Dread O - cean, haste with all thy streames: And, if you can - not quench my fire, O drowne both mee, O drowne both mee and my de - sire. -sire.

XXVI

Silly boy, 'tis ful Moone yet, thy night as day shines
$\qquad$ clearely;
Had thy youth but wit to feare, thou couldst not love
$\qquad$ so dearely.
Shortly wilt thou mourne when all thy pleasures are
$\qquad$ bereaved;
Little knowes he how to love that never was deceived.

This is thy first mayden flame, that triumphes yet
$\qquad$ unstayned;
All is artlesse now you speake, not one word yet is
$\qquad$ fayned;
All is heav'n that you behold, and all your thoughts are
$\qquad$ blessed:
But no Spring can want his Fall, each *Troylus* hath his
$\qquad$ *Cresseid.*

Thy well-order'd lockes ere long shall rudely hang
$\qquad$ neglected;
And thy lively pleasant cheare reade griefe on earth
$\qquad$ dejected.
Much then wilt thou blame thy Saint, that made thy
$\qquad$ heart so holy,
And with sighs confesse, in love, that too much faith is
$\qquad$ folly.

Yet, be just and constant still; Love may beget a wonder,
Not unlike a Summers frost, or Winters fatall thunder:
Hee that holds his Sweet-hart true unto his day of dying
Lives, of all that ever breath'd, most worthy the envying.

XXVIII

So quicke, so hot, so mad is thy fond sute,
So rude, so tedious growne, in urging mee,
That faine I would with losse make thy tongue mute,
And yeeld some little grace to quiet thee:
    An houre with thee I care not to converse,
    For I would not be counted too perverse.

But roofes too hot would prove for men all fire,
And hils too high for my unused pace;
The grove is charg'd with thornes and the bold bryer;
Gray Snakes the meadowes shrowde in every place:
    A yellow Frog, alas, will fright me so,
    As I should start and tremble as I goe.

Since then I can on earth no fit roome finde,
In heaven I am resolv'd with you to meete;
Till then, for Hopes sweet sake, rest your tir'd minde,
And not so much as see mee in the streete:
    A heavenly meeting one day wee shall have,
    But never, as you dreame, in bed, or grave.

So quicke, so hot, so mad is thy fond
That faine I would with losse make thy tongue

sute, So rude, so te - - dious growne, in urg-ing mee,
mute, And yeeld some lit - - tle grace to qui-et thee:

An houre with thee I care not to con - verse, (For

I would not be count - - ed too per - verse.

VII

To his sweet Lute *Apollo* sung the motions of the Spheares,
The wondrous order of the Stars, whose course divides the
yeares,
And all the Mysteries above:
But none of this could *Midas* move,
Which purchast him his Asses eares.

Then *Pan* with his rude Pipe began the Country-wealth
t'advance,
To boast of Cattle, flockes of Sheepe, and Goates on hils
that dance,
With much more of this churlish kinde:
That quite transported *Midas* minde,
And held him rapt as in a trance.

This wrong the *God of Musicke* scorn'd from such a sottish
Judge,
And bent his angry bow at *Pan*, which made the Piper
trudge:
Then *Midas* head he so did trim
That ev'ry age yet talkes of him
And *Phoebus* right revenged grudge.

To— his— sweet Lute A - pol - lo— sung the— mo-tions of the Spheares,

The won - - drous or - der of the Stars, whose course di - vides the yeares,

And all the Mys - ter-ies a - bove: But none of— this could Mi - das

move, Which pur - - - chast him his Ass - es eares.

X

Love me or not, love her I must or dye;
Leave me or not, follow her needs must I.
O, that her grace would my wisht comforts give:
How rich in her, how happy should I live!

All my desire, all my delight should be
Her to enjoy, her to unite to mee:
Envy should cease, her would I love alone:
Who loves by lookes, is seldome true to one.

Could I enchant, and that it lawfull were,
Her would I charme softly that none should heare.
But love enforc'd rarely yeelds firme content;
So would I love that neyther should repent.

Love   me or   not,   love   her I   must   or   dye;
Leave   me or   not,   fol - - low her   needs   must   I.

O,   that her   grace   would   my wisht com - - forts   give:

How rich   in   her,   how hap - py   should I   live!

XVIII

Think'st thou to seduce me then with words that have no
meaning?
Parats so can learne to prate, our speech by pieces gleaning:
Nurces teach their children so about the time of weaning.

Learne to speake first, then to wooe: to wooing much
pertayneth:
Hee that courts us, wanting Arte, soone falters when he
fayneth,
Lookes a-squint on his discourse, and smiles when hee
complaineth.

Skilfull Anglers hide their hookes, fit baytes for every
season;
But with crooked pins fish thou, as babes doe that want
reason;
Gogians onely can be caught with such poore trickes of
treason.

Ruth forgive me, if I err'd from humane hearts compassion
When I laught sometimes too much to see thy foolish
fashion:
But, alas, who lesse could doe that found so good occasion?

Thinkst thou to se - duce me then with words that have no
mean - ing? Pa - rats so can learne to prate, our
Nur - ces teach their chil - dren so a -
speech by piec - es glean - - ing.
- bout the time of wean - - - ing.

[99]

XXIII

Your faire lookes urge my desire:
   Calme it, sweet, with love.
Stay, o why will you retire?
   Can you churlish prove?
If Love may perswade,
   Loves pleasures, deare, deny not:
Here is a grove secur'd with shade;
   O then be wise, and flye not.

Harke, the Birds delighted sing,
   Yet our pleasure sleepes.
Wealth to none can profit bring,
   Which the miser keepes:
O come, while we may,
   Let's chayne Love with embraces;
Wee have not all times time to stay,
   Nor safety in all places.

What ill finde you now in this?
   Or who can complaine?
There is nothing done amisse,
   That breedes no man payne.
'Tis now flowry *May*,
   But ev'n in cold *December*,
When all these leaves are blowne away,
   This place shall I remember.

XXIIII

Faine would I wed a faire yong man that day and night
         could please mee,
When my mind or body grieved, that had the powre to ease
         mee.
Maids are full of longing thoughts that breed a bloudlesse
         sickenesse,
And that, oft I heare men say, is onely cur'd by quicknesse.
Oft have I beene woo'd and prai'd, but never could be
         moved:
Many for a day or so I have most dearely loved,
But this foolish mind of mine straight loaths the thing
         resolved.
If to love be sinne in mee, that sinne is soone absolved.
Sure, I thinke I shall at last flye to some holy Order;
When I once am setled there, then can I flye no farther.
Yet I would not dye a maid, because I had a mother:
As I was by one brought forth, I would bring forth another.

From
Observations in the Art of English Poesie

THE THIRD EPIGRAMME

Kate can fancy only berdles husbands,
Thats the cause she shakes off ev'ry suter,
Thats the cause she lives so stale a virgin,
For, before her heart can heate her answer,
Her smooth youths she finds all hugely berded.

THE EIGHT EPIGRAMME

Barnzy stiffly vowes that hees no Cuckold,
Yet the vulgar ev'rywhere salutes him
With strange signes of hornes, from ev'ry corner;
Wheresoere he commes, a sundry Cucco
Still frequents his eares; yet hees no Cuccold.
But this *Barnzy* knowes that his *Matilda*,
Skorning him, with *Harvy* playes the wanton.
Knowes it? nay desires it, and by prayers
Dayly begs of heav'n, that it for ever
May stand firme for him; yet hees no Cuccold.
And tis true, for *Harvy* keeps *Matilda*,
Fosters *Barnzy*, and relieves his houshold,
Buyes the Cradle, and begets the children,
Payes the Nurces, ev'ry charge defraying,
And thus truly playes *Matildas* husband:
So that *Barnzy* now becomes a cypher,
And himselfe th' adultrer of *Matilda*.
Mock not him with hornes, the case is alterd;
Harvy beares the wrong, he proves the Cuccold.

Rose-cheekt *Lawra*, come,
Sing thou smoothly with thy beawties
Silent musick, either other
Sweetely gracing.

Lovely formes do flowe
From concent devinely framed;
Heav'n is musick, and thy beawties
Birth is heavenly.

These dull notes we sing
Discords neede for helps to grace them;
Only beawty purely loving
Knowes no discord:

But still mooves delight,
Like cleare springs renu'd by flowing,
Ever perfect, ever in them-
selves eternall.

Just beguiler,
Kindest love, yet only chastest,
Royall in thy smooth denyals,
Frowning or demurely smiling,
Still my pure delight.

Let me view thee
With thoughts and with eyes affected,
And if then the flames do murmur,
Quench them with thy vertue, charme them
With thy stormy browes.

Heav'n so cheerefull
Laughs not ever, hory winter
Knowes his season, even the freshest
Sommer mornes from angry thunder
Jet not still secure.

Follow, followe,
Though with mischiefe
Arm'd, like whirlewind,
Now she flys thee;
Time can conquer
Loves unkindnes;
Love can alter
Times disgraces;
Till death faint not
Then, but followe.
Could I catch that
Nimble trayter,
Skornefull *Lawra,*
Swift foote *Lawra,*
Soone then would I
Seeke avengement.
Whats th' avengement?
Even submissely
Prostrate then to
Beg for mercye.

From

A Booke of Ayres

PART TWO

III

No grave for woe, yet earth my watrie teares devoures;
Sighes want ayre, and burnt desires kind pitties showres:
Stars hold their fatal course, my joies preventing:
The earth, the sea, the aire, the fire, the heav'ns vow my
                                                  tormenting.

Yet still I live, and waste my wearie daies in grones,
And with wofull tunes adorne dispayring mones.
Night still prepares a more displeasing morrow;
My day is night, my life my death, and all but sence of
                                                  sorrow.

XII

Shal I come, if I swim? wide are the waves, you see:
  Shall I come, if I flie, my deere love, to thee?
Streames Venus will appease, Cupid gives me winges:
  All the powers assist my desire
Save you alone, that set my wofull heart on fire.

You are faire; so was Hero that in Sestos dwelt;
  She a priest, yet the heate of love truly felt.
A greater streame then this did her love devide,
  But she was his guide with a light:
So through the streames Leander did enjoy her sight.

XV

If I hope, I pine; if I feare, I faint and die;
  So betweene hope and feare I desp'rat lie,
Looking for joy to heaven, whence it should come:
  But hope is blinde, joy deafe, and I am dumbe.

Yet I speake and crie, but alas with words of wo;
  And joy conceives not them that murmure so.
He that the eares of joy will ever pearse
  Must sing glad noates, or speake in happier verse.

XIX

Kinde in unkindnesse, when will you relent
And cease with faint love true love to torment?
Still entertain'd, excluded still I stand,
Her glove stil holde, but cannot touch the hand.

In her faire hand my hopes and comforts rest:
O might my fortunes with that hand be blest,
No envious breaths then my deserts could shake,
For they are good whom such true love doth make.

O let not beautie so forget her birth
That it should fruitles home returne to earth:
Love is the fruite of beautie, then love one;
Not your sweete selfe, for such selfe love is none.

Love one that onely lives in loving you,
Whose wrong'd deserts would you with pity view:
This strange distast which your affections swaies
Would relish love, and you find better daies.

Thus till my happie sight your beautie viewes,
Whose sweet remembrance stil my hope renewes,
Let these poore lines sollicite love for mee,
And place my joyes where my desires would bee.

XXI

Whether men doe laugh or weepe,
Whether they doe wake or sleepe,
Whether they die yoong or olde,
Whether they feele heate or colde,
There is, underneath the sunne,
Nothing in true earnest done.

All our pride is but a jest;
None are worst, and none are best;
Griefe, and joy, and hope, and feare
Play their Pageants every where:
Vaine opinion all doth sway,
And the world is but a play.

Powers above in cloudes doe sit,
Mocking our poore apish wit
That so lamely, with such state,
Their high glorie imitate:
No ill can be felt but paine,
And that happie men disdaine.

FINIS

THE LORDS MASKE

THE DESCRIPTION,
SPEECHES, AND SONGS, OF
THE LORDS MASKE, PRESENTED IN
the Banquetting-house on the mariage night
of the high and mightie Count Palatine,
and the royally descended the Ladie
ELISABETH

I have now taken occasion to satisfie many who long since were desirous that the Lords maske should be published, which, but for some private lets, had in due time come forth. The Scene was divided into two parts from the roofe to the floore; the lower part being first discovered (upon the sound of a double consort, exprest by severall instruments, plac't on either side of the roome), there appeared a Wood in prospective, the innermost part being of releave or whole round, the rest painted. On the left hand from the seate was a Cave, and on the right a thicket, out of which came Orpheus, *who was attired after the old Greeke manner, his haire curled and long; a lawrell wreath on his head; and in his hand hee bare a silver bird; about him tamely placed severall wild beasts; and upon the ceasing of the Consort* Orpheus *spake.*

ORPHEUS. Agen, agen, fresh kindle *Phoebus* sounds,
    T' exhale *Mania* from her earthie den;
  Allay the furie that her sense confounds,
    And call her gently forth; sound, sound agen.

The Consorts both sound againe, and Mania *the Goddesse of madnesse appears wildly out of her cave. Her habit was confused and strange, but yet gracefull; shee as one amazed speaks.*

MANIA. What powerfull noise is this importunes me,
    T' abandon darkenesse which my humour fits?
  Joves hand in it I feele, and ever he
    Must be obai'd, ev'n of the franticst wits.

ORPH. *Mania!*

MANIA. Hah.

ORPH. Braine-sick, why start'st thou so?
    Approch yet nearer, and thou then shalt know
    The will of *Jove*, which he will breath from me.

MANIA. Who art thou? if my dazeled eyes can see,
    Thou art the sweet Enchanter heav'nly *Orpheus*.

ORPH. The same, *Mania*, and *Jove* greets thee thus:
    Though severall power to thee, and charge he gave,
    T' enclose in thy Dominions such as rave
    Through blouds distemper, how durst thou attempt
    T' imprison *Entheus*, whose rage is exempt
    From vulgar censure? it is all divine,
    Full of celestiall rapture, that can shine
    Through darkest shadowes: therefore *Jove* by me
    Commands thy power strait to set *Entheus* free.

MANIA. How can I? Franticks with him many more
    In one cave are lockt up; ope once the dore,
    All will flie out, and through the world disturbe
    The peace of *Jove*; for what power then can curbe
    Their rainelesse furie? —

ORPH. — Let not feare in vaine
    Trouble thy crazed fancie; all againe,
    Save *Entheus*, to thy safeguard shall retire;
    For *Jove* into our musick will inspire
    The power of passion, that their thoughts shall bend
    To any forme or motion we intend.
    Obey *Joves* will then; go, set *Entheus* free.

MANIA. I willing go, so *Jove* obey'd must bee.

ORPH. Let Musicke put on *Protean* changes now;
    Wilde beasts it once tam'd, now let Franticks bow.

*At the sound of a strange musicke twelve Franticks enter, six
men and six women, all presented in sundry habits and humours:
there was the Lover, the Selfe-lover, the melancholicke-man full
of feare, the Schoole-man over-come with phantasie, the over-*

watched Usurer, with others that made an absolute medly of mad-
nesse; in middest of whom Entheus (*or Poeticke furie*) *was hurried*
forth, and tost up and downe, till by vertue of a new change in the
musicke, the Lunatickes fell into a madde measure, fitted to a loud
phantasticke tune; but in the end thereof the musicke changed into
a very solemne ayre, which they softly played, while Orpheus
spake.

ORPH. Through these soft and calme sounds, *Mania,* passe
    With thy Phantasticks hence; heere is no place
    Longer for them or thee; *Entheus* alone
    Must do *Joves* bidding now, all else be gone.

During this speech Mania *with her Franticks depart, leaving*
Entheus *behind them, who was attired in a close Curace of the*
Anticke fashion, Bases with labels, a Roabe fastned to his
shoulders, and hanging downe behind; on his head a wreath of
Lawrell, out of which grew a paire of wings; in the one hand he
held a booke, and in the other a pen.

ENTH. Divinest *Orpheus,* o how all from thee
    Proceed with wondrous sweetnesse! Am I free?
    Is my affliction vanisht?

ORPH. — Too too long,
    Alas, good *Entheus,* hast thou brook't this wrong;
    What? number thee with madmen? o mad age,
    Sencelesse of thee, and thy celestiall rage.
    For thy excelling rapture, ev'n through things
    That seems most light, is borne with sacred wings:
    Nor are these Musicks, Showes, or Revels vaine,
    When thou adorn'st them with thy *Phoebean* braine.
    Th' are pallate sick of much more vanitie,
    That cannot taste them in their dignitie.
    Jove therefore lets thy prison'd spright obtaine
    Her libertie and fiery scope againe:
    And heere by me commands thee to create
    Inventions rare, this night to celebrate,

[123]

Such as become a nuptiall by his will
Begun and ended. —

ENTH. — *Jove* I honor still,
And must obey. *Orpheus*, I feele the fires
Are reddy in my braine, which *Jove* enspires.
Loe, through that vaile, I see *Prometheus* stand
Before those glorious lights, which his false hand
Stole out of heav'n, the dull earth to enflame
With the affects of Love, and honor'd Fame.
I view them plaine in pompe and majestie,
Such as being seene might hold rivalitie
With the best triumphes. *Orpheus*, give a call
With thy charm'd musicke, and discover all.

ORPH. Flie, cheerfull voices, through the ayre, and clear
These clouds, that yon hid beautie may appeare.

A SONG

I

Come away; bring thy golden theft,
  Bring, bright *Prometheus*, all thy lights;
Thy fires from Heav'n bereft
  Shew now to humane sights.
Come quickly, come: thy stars to our stars straight
                         present,
For pleasure, being too much defer'd, loseth her best
                         content.
What fair dames wish should swift as their own thoughts
                         appeare;
To loving and to longing harts every houre seemes a
                         yeare.

2

See how faire: O how faire they shine;
  What yeelds more pompe beneath the skies?

[124]

Their birth is yet divine,
   And such their forme implies.
Large grow their beames, their nere approch afford them
                                        so;
By nature sights that pleasing are, cannot too amply show.
O might these flames in humane shapes descend this place,
How lovely would their presence be, how full of grace!

In the end of the first part of this Song, the upper part of the
Scene was discovered by the sodaine fall of a curtaine; then in
clowdes of severall colours (the upper part of them being fierie, and
the middle heightned with silver) appeared eight Starres of extraor-
dinarie bignesse, which so were placed as that they seemed to be
fixed betweene the Firmament and the Earth; in the front of the
Scene stood Prometheus, *attyred as one of the ancient Heroes.*

ENTH. Patron of mankinde, powerfull and bounteous,
   Rich in thy flames, reverend *Prometheus,*
   In *Hymens* place aide us to solempnize
   These royall Nuptials; fill the lookers eyes
   With admiration of thy fire and light,
   And from thy hand let wonders flow tonight.

PROM. *Entheus* and *Orpheus,* names both deare to me,
   In equall ballance I your Third will be
   In this nights honour. View these heav'n borne Starres,
   Who by my stealth are become Sublunars;
   How well their native beauties fit this place,
   Which with a chorall dance they first shall grace;
   Then shall their formes to humane figures turne,
   And these bright fires within their bosomes burne.
   Orpheus, apply thy musick, for it well
   Helps to induce a Courtly miracle.

ORPH. Sound, best of Musicks, raise yet higher our sprights,
   While we admire *Prometheus* dancing lights.

[125]

A SONG

1

Advance your Chorall motions now,
   You musick-loving lights;
This night concludes the nuptiall vow,
   Make this the best of nights:
So bravely Crowne it with your beames,
   That it may live in fame,
As long as *Rhenus* or the *Thames*
   Are knowne by either name.

2

Once move againe, yet nearer move
   Your formes at willing view;
Such faire effects of joy and love
   None can expresse but you:
Then revel midst your ayrie Bowres
   Till all the clouds doe sweat,
That pleasure may be powr'd in showres
   On this triumphant Seat.

3

Long since hath lovely *Flora* throwne
   Her Flowers and Garlands here;
Rich *Ceres* all her wealth hath showne,
   Prowde of her daintie cheare.
Chang'd then to humane shape, descend,
   Clad in familiar weede,
That every eye may here commend
   The kinde delights you breede.

According to the humour of this Song, the Starres mooved in an exceeding strange and delightfull maner; and I suppose fewe have ever seene more neate artifice then Master Innigoe Jones *shewed in contriving their Motion, who in all the rest of the work-manship which belong'd to the whole invention shewed extraordi-narie industrie and skill; which if it be not as lively exprest in writing as it appeared in view, robbe not him of his due, but lay the blame on my want of right apprehending his instructions for the adoring of his Arte. But to returne to our purpose: about the end of this Song, the Starres suddainely vanished, as if they had beene drowned amongst the Cloudes, and the eight Maskers appeared in their habits, which were infinitly rich, befitting States (such as indeede they all were), as also a time so farre heightned the day before with all the richest shew of solemnitie that could be invented. The ground of their attires was massie Cloth of Silver, embossed with flames of Embroidery; on their heads they had Crownes, Flames made all of Gold-plate Enameled, and on the top a Feather of Silke, representing a cloude of smoake. Upon their new transformation, the whole Scaene being Cloudes dispers-ed, and there appeared an Element of artificiall fires, with severall circles of lights, in continuall motion, representing the house of Prometheus, who thus applies his speech to the Maskers.*

They are transformed.

PROM. So pause awhile, and come, yee fierie spirits,
  Breake forth the earth like sparks t'attend these Knights.

Sixteene Pages like fierie spirits, all their attires being alike composed of flames, with fierie Wings and Bases, bearing in either hand a Torch of Virgine Waxe, come forth below dauncing a lively measure; and the Daunce being ended, Prometheus speakes to them from above.

THE TORCH-BEARERS DAUNCE

PROM. Wait, spirits, wait, while through the clouds we pace,
  And by descending gaine a hier place.

The Pages returne toward the Scaene, to give their attendance to the Maskers with their light: from the side of the Scaene ap-

[127]

peared a bright and transparant cloud, which reached from the top of the heavens to the earth; on this cloud the Maskers led by Prometheus *descended with the musicke of a full song; and at the end of their descent the cloud brake in twaine, and one part of it (as with a winde) was blowne overthwart the Scaene.*

While this cloud was vanishing, the wood being the underpart of the Scaene was insensibly changed, and in place thereof appeared foure Noble women-statues of silver, standing in severall nices, accompanied with ornaments of Architecture which filled all the end of the house, and seemed to be all of gold-smithes work. The first order consisted of Pillasters all of gold, set with Rubies, Saphyrs, Emeralds, Opals, and such like. The Capitels were composed, and of a new invention. Over this was a bastard order with Cartouses reversed, comming from the Capitels of every Pillaster, which made the upper part rich and full of ornament. Over every statue was placed a history in gold, which seemed to be of base releave; the conceits which were figured in them were these. In the first was Prometheus, *embossing in clay the figure of a woman; in the second he was represented stealing fire from the chariot-wheele of the Sunne; in the third he is exprest putting life with this fire into his figure of clay; and in the fourth square,* Jupiter, *enraged, turnes these new made women into statues. Above all, for finishing, ran a Cornish, which returned over every Pillaster, seeming all of gold and richly carved.*

A FULL SONG

Supported now by Clouds descend,
Divine *Prometheus,* *Hymens* friend:
Leade downe the new transformed fires,
And fill their breasts with loves desires;
That they may revell with delight,
And celebrate this nuptiall night,
So celebrate this nuptiall night,
   That all which see may stay:

They never viewed so faire a sight,
　　Even on the cleerest day.

ENTH. See, see, *Prometheus:* four of these first dames
　Which thou long since out of thy purchac't flames
　Did'st forge with heav'nly fire, as they were then
　By *Jove* transformed to Statues, so agen
　They suddenly appeare by his command
　At thy arrivall. Loe, how fixt they stand;
　So did *Joves* wrath too long, but now at last
　It by degrees relents, and he hath plac't
　These Statues, that we might his ayde implore,
　First for the life of these, and then for more.

PROM. *Entheus,* thy councels are divine and just;
　Let *Orpheus* decke thy Hymne, since pray we must.

THE FIRST INVOCATION IN A FULL SONG

　　Powerfull *Jove,* that of bright starres
　　Now hast made men fit for warres,
　　Thy power in these Statues prove,
　　And make them women fit for love.

ORPH. See, *Jove* is pleas'd; Statues have life and move:
　Go, new-borne men, and entertaine with love
　These new-borne women; though your number yet
　Exceedes their's double, they are arm'd with wit
　To beare your best encounters. Court them faire:
　When words and Musicke speake, let none despaire.

THE SONG

I

　Wooe her, and win her, he that can:
　　Each woman hath two lovers,
　So shee must take and leave a man,

Till time more grace discovers;
This doth *Jove* to shew that want
    Makes beautie most respected;
If faire women were more skant,
    They would be more affected.

2

Courtship and Musicke suite with love,
    They both are workes of passion;
Happie is he whose words can move,
    Yet sweete notes helpe perswasion.
Mixe your words with Musicke then,
    That they the more may enter;
Bold assaults are fit for men,
    That on strange beauties venture.

While this Song is sung, and the Maskers court the fowre new transformed Ladies, foure other Statues appeare in their places.

PROM. Cease, cease your woing strife; see, *Jove* intends
    To fill your number up, and make all friends.
    Orpheus and *Entheus*, joyne your skils once more,
    And with a Hymne the Dietie implore.

THE SECOND INVOCATION TO THE TUNE OF THE FIRST

Powerfull *Jove*, that hast given fower,
Raise this number but once more,
That, complete, their numerous feet
May aptly in just measures meet.

The other foure statues are transformed into women, in the time of this invocation.

ENTH. The number's now complete, thankes be to *Jove*:
    No man needs fear a Rivall in his love;

For, all are sped, and now begins delight
To fill with glorie this triumphant night.

*The Maskers, having every one entertained his Lady, begin
their first new entring dance; after it, while they breath, the time
is entertained with a dialogue song.*

Breath you now, while Io Hymen
 To the Bride we sing:
O how many joyes, and honors,
 From this match will spring!
Ever firme the league will prove,
Where only goodnesse causeth love.
Some for profit seeke
What their fancies most disleeke:
The love for vertues sake alone:
Beautie and youth unite them both in one.
CHORUS.
Live with thy Bridegroome happy, sacred Bride;
How blest is he that is for love envi'd.

THE MASKERS SECOND DANCE

Breath againe, while we with musicke
 Fill the emptie space:
O but do not in your dances
 Your selves only grace.
Ev'ry one fetch out your *Pheare*,
Whom chiefely you will honor heere.
Sights most pleasure breed,
When their numbers most exceed:
Chuse then, for choice to all is free;
Taken or left, none discontent must bee.
CHORUS.
Now in thy Revels frolicke-faire delight,
To heap Joy on this ever honored night.

[131]

*The Maskers during this Dialogue take out others to daunce
with them, men women, and women men; and first of all the
Princely Bridegroome and Bride were drawne into these solemne
Revels, which continued a long space, but in the end were broken
off with this short Song.*

A SONG

Cease, cease you Revels, rest a space;
New pleasures presse into this place,
Full of beautie and of grace.

*The whole scaene was now againe changed, and became a
prospective with Porticoes on each side, which seemed to go in a
great way; in the middle was erected an Obeliske, all of silver, and
in it lights of severall colours; on the side of this Obeliske, standing
on Pedestals, were the statues of the Bridegroome and Bride, all of
gold in gratious postures. This Obeliske was of that height, that
the toppe thereof touched the highest cloudes, and yet* Sybilla *did
draw it forth with a threed of gold. The grave* Sage *was in a
Roabe of gold tuckt up before to her girdle, a Kirtle gathered full,
and of silver; with a vaile on her head, being bare-neckt, and
bearing in her hand a scrole of Parchment.*

ENTH. Make cleare the passage to *Sibilla's* sight,
Who with her Trophee comes, to crowne this night;
And, as her selfe with Musicke shall be led,
So shall shee pull on with a golden thread
A high vast *Obeliske*, dedicate to fame,
Which immortalitie it selfe did frame.
Raise high your voices now; like Trumpets fill
The roome with sounds of Triumph, sweete and shrill.

A SONG

Come triumphing, come with state,
Old *Sibilla*, reverend Dame;

Thou keep'st the secret key of fate,
　　Preventing swiftest fame.
This night breath onely words of joy,
And speake them plaine, now be not coy.

SYBILLA. Debetur alto iure Principium Iovi,
　　Votis det ipse vim meis, dictis fidem.
　　Utrinque decoris splendet egregium Iubar;
　　Medio triumphus mole stat dignus sua,
　　Caelumque summo Capite dilectum petit.
　　Quam pulchra pulchro sponsa respondet viro!
　　Quam plena numinis! Patrem vultu exprimit,
　　Parens futura masculae prolis, Parens
　　Regum, imperatorum. Additur Germaniae
　　Robur Britannicum: ecquid esse par potest?
　　Utramque iunget una mens gentem, fides,
　　Deique Cultus unus, et simplex amor.
　　Idem erit utrique hostis, sodalis idem, idem
　　Votum periclitantium, atque eadem manus.
　　Favebit illis Pax, favebit bellica
　　Fortuna, semper aderit Adiutor Deus.
　　Sic, sic Sibilla; vocibus nec his deest
　　Pondus, nec hoc inane monumentum trahit.
　　Et aureum est, et quale nec flammas timet,
　　Nec fulgura, ipsi quippe sacratur Jovi.

PROM. The good old *Sage* is silenc't; her free tongue,
　　That made such melodie, is now unstrung:
　　Then grace her Trophee with a dance triumphant;
　　Where *Orpheus* is, none can fit musick want.

[133]

A SONG AND DANCE TRIUMPHANT
OF THE MASKERS

1

Dance, dance, and visit now the shadowes of our joy,
All in height, and pleasing state, your changed formes
imploy.
And as the bird of *Jove* salutes, with loftie wing, the morn,
So mount, so flie, these Trophees to adorne.
Grace them with all the sounds and motions of delight,
Since all the earth cannot expresse a lovelier sight.
View them with triumph, and in shades the truth adore:
No pompe or sacrifice can please *Ioves* greatnesse more.

2

Turne, turne, and honor now the life these figures beare;
Loe, how heav'nly natures farre above all art appeare;
Let their aspects revive in you the fire that shin'd so late,
Still mount and still retaine your heavenly state.
Gods were with dance, and with musick serv'd of old,
Those happy daies deriv'd their glorious stile from gold:
This pair, by *Hymen joyn'd*, grace you with measures then,
Since they are both divine, and you are more then men.

ORPH. Let here *Sybilla's* Trophee stand,
   Leade her now by either hand,
   That shee may approch yet nearer,
   And the Bride and Bridegroome heare her
   Blesse them in her native tongue,
   Wherein old prophesies shee sung,
   Which time to light hath brought:
   Shee speakes that which *Jove* hath taught:
   Well may he inspire her now,
   To make a joyfull and true vow.

SYB. Sponsam sponse toro tene pudicam,
Sponsum sponsa tene toro pudicum.
Non haec unica nox datur beatis,
At vos perpetuo haec beabit una
Prole multiplici, parique amore.
Laeta, ac vera refert Sybilla; ab alto
Ipse Iuppiter annuit loquenti.

PROM. So be it ever, joy and peace,
And mutuall love give you increase,
That your posteritie may grow
In fame, as long as Seas doe flow.

ENTH. Live you long to see your joyes,
In faire Nymphs and Princely Boyes;
Breeding like the Garden flowers,
Which kinde heav'n drawes with her warme showers.

ORPH. Enough of blessing, though too much
Never can be said to such;
But night doth wast, and *Hymen* chides,
Kinde to Bridegroomes and to Brides.
Then, singing, the last dance induce,
So let good night prevent excuse.

THE SONG

No longer wrong the night
Of her *Hymenaean* right;
A thousand *Cupids* call away,
Fearing the approching day;
The Cocks alreadie crow:
Dance then and goe.

The last new Dance of the Maskers, which concludes
all with a lively straine at their going out.

[135]

FACSIMILES
from the
Bookes of Ayres

I.

Y sweetest Lesbia let vs liue and loue, and though the sager sort our

deedes re-proue, let vs not way them heau'ns great lampes doe diue into their west, and

strait againe re-uiue, but soone as once set is our little light, then must we sleepe one

euer-during night, euer-during night.

If all would lead their liues in loue like mee,
Then bloudie swords and armour should not be,
No drum nor trumpet peaceful sleepes should moue,
Vnles alar'me came from the campe of loue :
But fooles do liue, and wast their little light,
And seeke with paine their euer during night.

When timely death my life and fortune ends,
Let not my hearse be vext with mourning friends,
But let all louers rich in triumph come,
And with sweet pastimes grace my happie tombe,
And Lesbia close vp thou my little light,
And crowne with loue my euer during night.

III.

I Care not for these Ladies that must be wooed and praide,
Giue me kind Amarillis the wanton country maide,
Nature art disdaineth, her beautie is her owne, Her when we court & kisse, she cries forsooth let go,
but when we come where comfort is she neuer will say no.

If I loue Amarillis,
She giues me fruit and flowers,
But if we loue these Ladies,
We must giue golden showers,
Giue them gold that sell loue,
Giue me the Nutbrowne lasse,
    VVho when we court, &c.

These Ladies must haue pillowes,
And beds by strangers wrought,
Giue me a Bower of willowes,
Of mosse and leaues vnbought.
And fresh Amarillis
With milke and honie fed,
    VVho when we court, &c.

IIII.

Ollowe thy faire sunne vnhappy shaddowe though

thou though thou be blacke as night and she made all of light, yet follow thy faire sunne vn-

hap- pie shaddowe.

Follow her whose light thy light depriueth,   Follow her while yet her glorie shineth,
Though here thou liu'st disgrac't,   There comes a luckles night,
And she in heauen is plac't,   That will dim all her light,
Yet follow her whose light the world reuiueth.   And this the black vnhappie shade deuineth.

Follow those pure beames whose beautie burneth,   Follow still since so thy fates ordained,
That so haue scorched thee,   The Sunne must haue his shade,
As thou still blacke must bee,   Till both at once doe fade,
Til her kind beames thy black to brightnes turneth.   The Sun still prou'd the shadow still disdained.

C

[141]

Vt of my soules depth to thee my cryes haue   sounded, Let thine eares my

plaints receiue on iust feare grounded : Lord should'st thou weigh our faults, who's not con-   founded?

1 Out of my soules deapth to thee my cryes haue sounded,
Let thine eares my plaints receiue on iust feare grounded :
Lord should'st thou weigh our faults, who's not confounded ?

2 But with grace thou censur'st thine when they haue erred,
Therefore shall thy blessed name belou'd and feared,
Eu'n to thy throne my thoughts and eyes are reared.

3 Thee alone my hopes attend, on thee relying ;
In thy sacred word I'le trust, to thee fast flying
Long ere the Watch shall breake, the morne descrying.

4 In the mercies of our God who liue secured,
May of full redemption rest in him assured,
Their sinne-sicke soules by him shall be recured.

Iew me Lord a worke of thine, Shall I then lye drown'd in night?Might thy grace in

me but shine, I should seeme made   all of light.

1 View mee Lord, a worke of thine ;
Shall I then lye drown'd in night?
Might thy grace in mee but shine,
I should seeme made all of light.

2 But my soule still surfets so
On the poysoned baytes of sinne,
That I strange and vgly growe,
All in darke, and foule within.

3 Clense mee Lord that I may kneele
At thine Altar pure and white,

They that once thy Mercies feele,
Gaze no more on earths delight.

4 Worldly ioyes like shadowes fade,
When the heau'nly light appeares,
But the cou'nants thou hast made
Endlesse, know nor dayes, nor yeares.

5 In thy word Lord is my trust,
To thy mercies fast I flye,
Though I am but clay and dust,
Yet thy grace can lift me high.

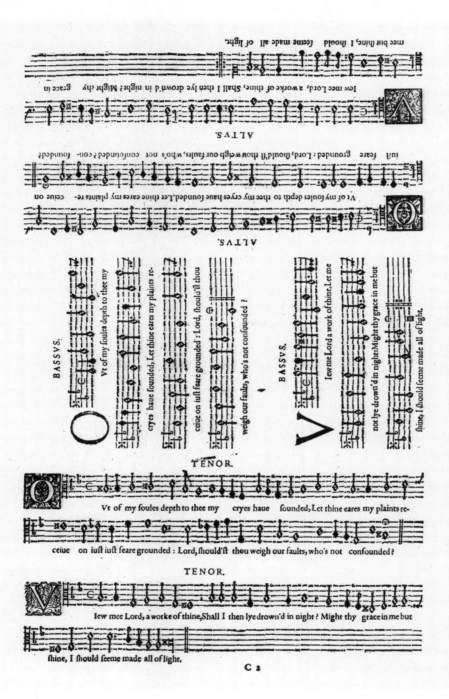

Raue-ly deckt, come forth bright day, thine houres with Roses strew thy way, as they
Thou re-ceiu'd shalt   be   with feasts, come chie- fest of the *Brit-tish* ghests, thou sift

wel remember: Thou w̄ triumph shalt exceed In the strictest ember, For by thy return the Lord records his blessed deed.
of *Nouember:*

1 Brauely deckt come forth bright day,
Thine houres with Roses strew thy way,
        As they well remember.
Thou receiu'd shalt be with feasts,
Come chiefest of the *British* ghests,
        Thou sift of *Nouember.*
Thou with triumph shalt exceede
        In the strictest ember ;
For by thy returne the Lord records his blessed deede.

2 *Britaines* frolicke at your bourd,
But first sing praises to the Lord
        In your Congregations.
Hee preseru'd your state alone,
His louing grace hath made you one
        Of his chosen Nations.
But this light must hallowed be
        With your best Oblations ;
Prayse the Lord, for onely great and mercifull is hee.

3 Death had enter'd in the gate,
And ruine was crept neare the State ;
        But heau'n all reuealed.
Fi'ry Powder hell did make,
Which ready long the flame to take,
        Lay in shade concealed.
God vs helpt of his free grace,
        None to him appealed ;
For none was so bad to feare the treason or the place.

4 God his peacefull Monarch chose,
To him the mist he did disclose,
        To him, and none other ;
This hee did O King for thee,
That thou thine owne renowne might'st see,
        Which no time can smother :
May blest *Charles* thy comfort be
        Firmer then his Brother,
May his heart the loue of peace, and wisedome learne from thee.

O Musicke bent is my re- ty-red mind, And fain would   I   some song of plea- sure sing :
But in vain ioies no cófort now I finde, From heauenly thoughts al true delight doth spring.

Thy power O God, thy mercies to record, Will sweeten euery note and euery word.

1 To Musicke bent is my retyred minde,
And faine would I some song of pleasure sing :
But in vaine ioyes no comfort now I finde :
From heau'nly thoughts all true delight doth spring.
Thy power O God, thy mercies to record
Will sweeten eu'ry note, and eu'ry word.

2 All earthly pompe or beauty to expresse,
Is but to carue in snow, on waues to writ :.
Celestiall things though men conceiue them lesse,
Yet fullest are they in themselues of light :
Such beames they yeeld as know no meanes to dye :
Such heate they cast as lifts the Spirit high.

O

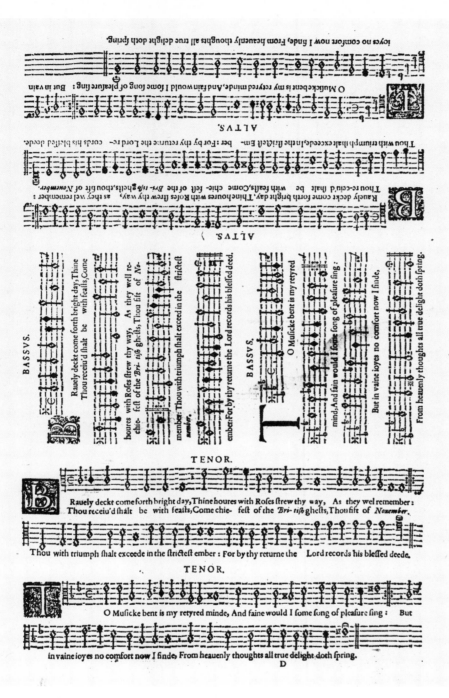

BASSVS.

Rauely deckt come forth bright day, Thine
Thou receiu'd shalt be with feasts, Come
houres with Roses strew thy way, As they well re-
chie- fest of the Bri- tish ghests, Thou sist of No-
member: Thou with triumph shalt exceed in the strictest
member.
ember: For by thy returne the Lord records his blessed deed.

BASSVS.

O Musicke bent is my retyred
mind, And fain would I some song of pleasure sing :
But in vaine ioyes no comfort now I finde,
From heauenly thoughts all true delight doth spring.

TENOR.

Rauely deckt come forth bright day, Thine houres with Roses strew thy way, As they wel remember :
Thou receiu'd shalt be with feasts, Come chie- fest of the *Bri- tish* ghests, Thou sist of *Nouember.*

Thou with triumph shalt exceede in the strictest ember : For by thy returne the Lord records his blessed deede.

TENOR.

O Musicke bent is my retyred minde, And faine would I some song of pleasure sing : But

in vaine ioyes no comfort now I finde, From heauenly thoughts all true delight doth spring.

D

Ife men patience neuer want, Good men pit- ty cannot hide, Hee alone for-
Fee-ble spirits onely vant Of reuenge, the poorest pride.

giue that can   Beares the true foule   of a man.

1 Wise men patience neuer want,
Good men pitty cannot hide :
Feeble spirits onely vant
Of reuenge, the poorest pride.
Hee alone forgiue that can
Beares the true foule of a man.

2 Some there are debate that feeke
Making trouble their content,
Happy if they wrong the mæeke,
Vexe them that to peace are bent ;
Such vndooe the common tye
Of mankinde, focietie.

3 Kindreffe growne is, latel , colde,
Con'cience hath forgot her pari :
Bleffed times were knowne of old,
Long ere Law became an Art.
Shame deterr'd, nor Statutes men,
Honeft loue was law to men.

4 Deeds from loue and words that flowe
Foster like kinde *April* fhowres ;
In the warme Sunne all things grow,
Wholfome fruits and pleafant flowres.
All fo thriues his gentle rayes,
Where on humane loue difplayes.

Euer weather-beaten faile more wil- ling bent to fhore, Then my weary fpright now
Neuer tyred pilgrims limbs af- fe- cted flumber more ;

longs to flye out of my troubled breft. O come quickly, O come quickly, O come quickly fweeteft Lord &

take my foule to reft.

1 Neuer weather-beaten Saile more willing bent to fhore,
Neuer tyred Pilgrims limbs affected flumber more ;
Then my weary fpright now longs to flye out of my troubled breft.
O come quickly fweeteft Lord, and take my foule to reft.

2 Euer-blooming are the ioyes of Heau'ns high paradice,
Cold age deafes not there our eares, nor vapour dims our eyes ;
Glory there the Sun out-fhines, whofe beames the bleffed onely fee:
O come quickly glorious Lord, and raife my fpright to thee.

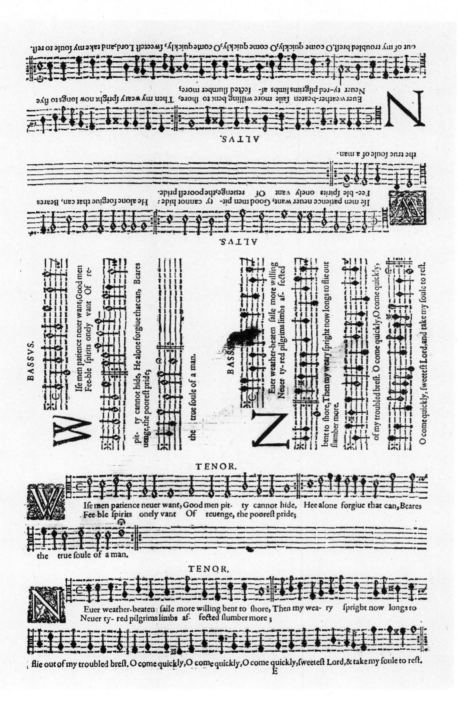

X.

Follow your Saint follow with accents sweet, There wrapt in cloud of
Haste you sad noates fall at her flying feete, But if she scorns my

sorrowe pitie moue, And tell the rauisher of my soule, I perish for her loue.
neuer ceasing paine, Then burst with sighing in her sight, And nere returne againe.

All that I soong still to her praise did tend,
Still she was first, still she my songs did end,
Yet she my loue, and Musicke both doeth flie,
The Musicke that her Eccho is, and beauties simpathie;
Then let my Noates pursue her scornefull flight,
It shall suffice, that they were breath'd, and dyed for her delight.

CANTVS.   XXI.

LL lookes be pale, harts cold as stone, For *Hally* now is dead and gone, *Hally* in whose sight, Most sweet sight, All the earth late tooke delight. Eu'ry eye weepe with me, weepe with me, weepe with me, Ioyes drown'd in teares must be, ioyes drown'd in teares must be.

1 All lookes be pale, harts cold as stone,
For *Hally* now is dead, and gone,
 Hally in whose sight,
 Most sweet sight,
All the earth late tooke delight.
Eu'ry eye weepe with mee,
Ioyes drown'd in teares must be.

2 His Iu'ry skin, his comely hayre,
His Rosie cheekes so cleare, and faire :
 Eyes that once did grace
 His bright face,
Now in lum all want their place.
Eyes and hearts weepe with mee,
For who so kinde as hee?

3 His youth was like an *Aprill* flowre,
Adorn'd with beauty, loue, and powre,
 Glory strow'd his way,
 Whose wreaths gay
Now are all turn'd to decay.
Then againe weepe with mee,
None feele more cause then wee.

4 No more may his wisht sight returne,
His golden Lampe no more can burne ;
 Quencht is all his flame,
 His hop't fame
Now hathl eft him nought but name.
For him all weepe with mee,
Since more him none shall see.

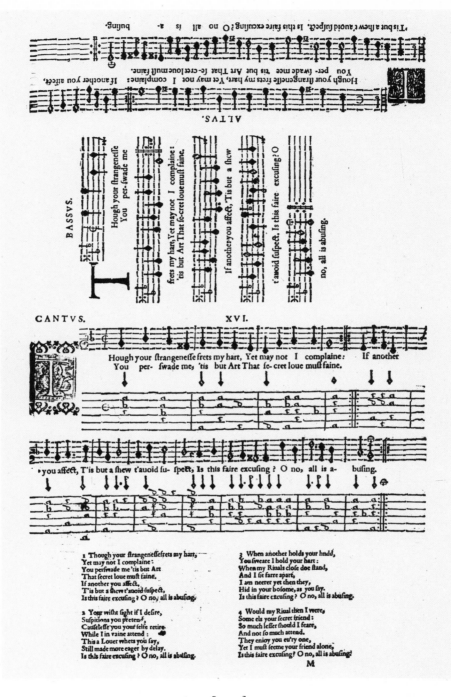

1 Though your strangenesse frets my hart,
Yet may not I complaine:
You perswade me 'tis but Art
That secret loue must faine.
If another you affect,
T'is but a shew t'auoid suspect,
Is this faire excusing? O no, all is abusing.

2 Your wisht sight if I desire,
Suspitions you pretend,
Causelesse you your selfe retire
While I in vaine attend:
This a Louer whets you say,
Still made more eager by delay.
Is this faire excusing? O no, all is abusing.

3 When another holds your hand,
You sweare I hold your hart:
When my Riuals close doe stand,
And I sit farre apart,
I am neerer yet then they,
Hid in your bosome, as you say.
Is this faire excusing? O no, all is abusing.

4 Would my Riual then I were,
Some els your secret friend:
So much lesser should I feare,
And not so much attend.
They enioy you eu'ry one,
Yet I must seeme your friend alone,
Is this faire excusing? O no, all is abusing?

M

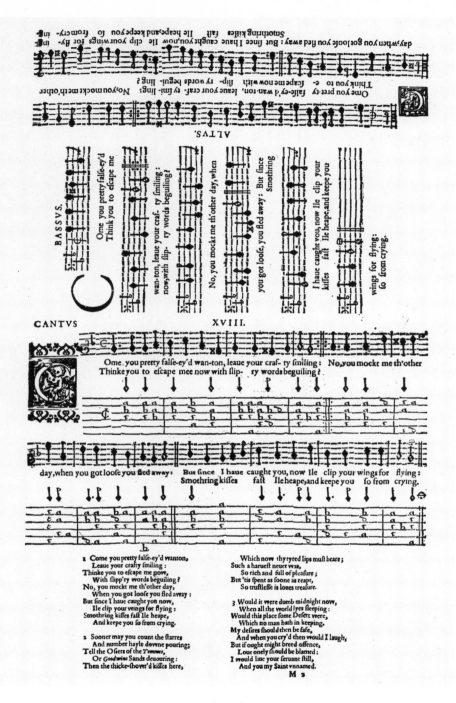

XVIII.

Ome, you pretty false-ey'd wan-ton, leaue your craf- ty smiling : No, you mockt me th'other
Thinke you to escape mee now with slip- ry words beguiling ?

day, when you got loose you fled away : But since I haue caught you, now Ile clip your wings for flying :
Smothring kisses fast Ile heape, and keepe you so from crying.

1 Come you pretty false-ey'd wanton,
    Leaue your crafty smiling :
Thinke you to escape me now,
    With slipp'ry words beguiling ?
No, you mockt me th'other day,
    When you got loose you fled away :
But since I haue caught you now,
    Ile clip your wings for flying :
Smothring kisses fast Ile heape,
    And keepe you so from crying.

2 Sooner may you count the starres
    And number hayle downe pouring;
Tell the Osiers of the Temmes,
    Or Goodwins Sands deuouring :
Then the thicke-showr'd kisses here,

Which now thy tyred lips must beare ;
    Such a haruest neuer was,
    So rich and full of pleasure ;
But 'tis spent as soone as reapt,
    So trustlesse is loues treasure.

3 Would it were dumb midnight now,
    When all the world lyes sleeping :
Would this place some Desert were,
    Which no man hath in keeping.
My desires should then be safe,
    And when you cry'd then would I laugh,
But if ought might breed offence,
    Loue onely should be blamed :
I would liue your seruant still,
    And you my Saint vnnamed.

M 2

[151]

Aydes are simple some men say, They forsooth will trust no men:

But should they mens wils o——bey, Maides were very simple then.

BASSVS.

2 Truth a rare flower now is growne,   Then a young mans vowes beleeue,
Few men weare it in their hearts;   When he sweares his loue is true.
Louers are more easily knowne
By their follies, then deserts.   2 Loue they make a poore blinde childe,
    But let none trust such as hee;
3 Safer may we credit giue   Rather then to be beguil'd
To a faithlesse wandring Iew,   Euer let me simple be.

CANTVS.   V.

O tyr'd are all my thoughts, that sence and spirits faile; Mourning I pine, and

know not what I ayle. O what can yeeld ease to a minde, ioy in nothing that can finde?

BASSVS.

1 How are my powres fore-spoke ? what strange distaste is this ?
Hence cruell hate of that which sweetest is :
Come, come delight, make my dull braine
    Feele once heate of ioy againe.

3 The louers teares are sweet, their mouer makes them so :
Proud of a wound the bleeding Souldiers grow :

Poore I alone, dreaming, endure
    Griefe that knowes nor cause, nor cure.

And whence can all this grow ? euen from an idle minde,
That no delight in any good can finde.
Action alone makes the soule blest;
    Vertue dyes with too much rest.

Ow winter nights en- large the number of their houres, And clouds their
Let now the chimneys blaze, and cups o'er- flow with wine: Let well tun'd

stormes dis- charge vp- on the ayrie towres, Now yel- low waxen lights shall waite on hunny
words a- maze with har-mo- nie di- uine.

Loue, While youthfull Reuels, Masks, and Courtly sights, sleepes leaden spels re- moue.

BASSVS.

2 · This time doth well dispence
    With louers long discourse ;
Much speech hath some defence,
    Though beauty no remorse.
All doe not all things well ;
    Some measures comely tread ;
Some knotted Ridles tell ;
    Some Poems smoothly read.
The Summer hath his ioyes,
    And Winter his delights ;
Though Loue and all his pleasures are but toyes,
    They shorten tedious nights.

C 2

[153]

Ire, fire, fire, fire, loe here I burne, I burne in such desire, That all.

the teares that I can straine out of mine idle empty braine, Cannot al- lay my scorching paine.

Come *Trent* and *Humber*, and fayre *Thames*, Dread Ocean haste with all thy streames: And

if you can- not quench my fire, O drowne both mee, O drowne both me, and my de- sire.

BASSVS.

2 Fire, fire, fire, fire.
There is no hell to my desire :
See all the Riuers backward flye,
And th' Ocean doth his waues deny,
For feare my heate should drinke them dry.
    Come heau'nly showres then pouring downe ;
    Come you that once the world did drowne :
    Some then you spar'd, but now saue all,
    That else must burne, and with mee fall.

O quicke, so hot, so mad is thy fond sute; So rude, so
That faine I would with losse make thy tongue mute, And yeeld some

te- dious growne in vrging mee. An houre with thee I care not to con- verse : For I would not
lit- tle grace to quiet thee.

be coun- ted too peruerse.

BASSVS.

2 But roofes too hot would proue for men all fire,
And hils too high for my vnused pace ;
The groue is charg'd with thornes and the bold bryer;
Gray Snakes the meadowes throwde in euery place :
    A yellow Frog alas will fright me so
    As I should start and tremble as I goe.

3 Since then I can on earth no fit roome finde,
In heauen I am resolu'd with you to meete ;
Till then for Hopes sweet sake rest your tir'd minde,
And not so much as see mee in the streete :
    A heauenly meeting one day wee shall haue,
    But neuer, as you dreame, in bed, or graue.

F 2

VIII.

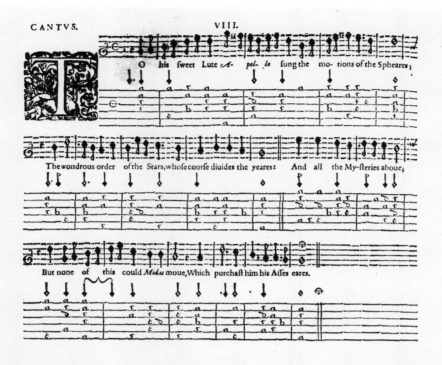

TO his sweet Lute Apollo sung the motions of the Spheares;
The wondrous order of the Stars, whose course diuides the yeares: And all the My-steries aboue;
But none of this could Midas moue, Which purchast him his Asses eares.

BASSVS.

2 Then *Pan* with his rude Pipe began the Country-wealth t'aduance ;
To boast of Cattle, flockes of Sheepe, and Goates, on hils that dance,
    With much more of this churlish kinde :
    That quite transported *Midas* minde,
    An held him rapt as in a trance.

3 This wrong the *God of Musicke* scorn'd from such a sottish Iudge,
And bent his angry bow at *Pan*, which made the *Piper* trudge:
    Then *Midas* head he so did trim,
    That eu'ry age yet talkes of him
    And *Phœbus* right reuenged grudge.

[157]

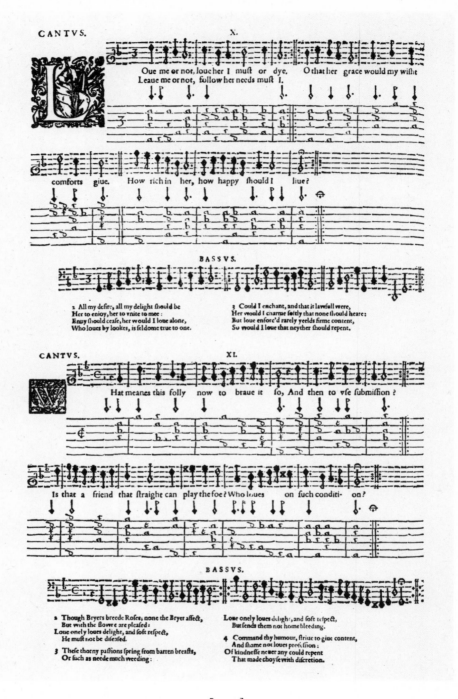

CANTVS.   X.

Oue me or not, loue her I must or dye,   O that her grace would my wisht
Leaue me or not, follow her needs must I.

comforts giue.   How rich in her, how happy should I liue?

BASSVS.

2 All my desire, all my delight should be   3 Could I enchant, and that it lawfull were,
Her to enioy, her to vnite to mee :   Her would I charme softly that none should heare:
Enuy should cease, her would I loue alone,   But loue enforc'd rarely yeelds firme content,
Who loues by lookes, is seldome true to one.   So would I loue that neyther should repent.

CANTVS.   XI.

Hat meanes this folly now to braue it   so, And then to vse submission?

Is that a friend that straight can play the foe? Who loues on such conditi- on?

BASSVS.

2 Though Bryers breede Roses, none the Bryer affect,   Loue onely loues delight, and soft respect,
But with the flowre are pleased :   But sends them not home bleeding.
Loue onely loues delight, and soft respect,
He must not be diseased.   4 Command thy humour, striue to giue content,
                                                     And shame not loues profession :
3 These thorny passions spring from barren breasts,   Of kindnesse neuer any could repent
Or such as neede much weeding :   That made choyse with discretion.

[158]

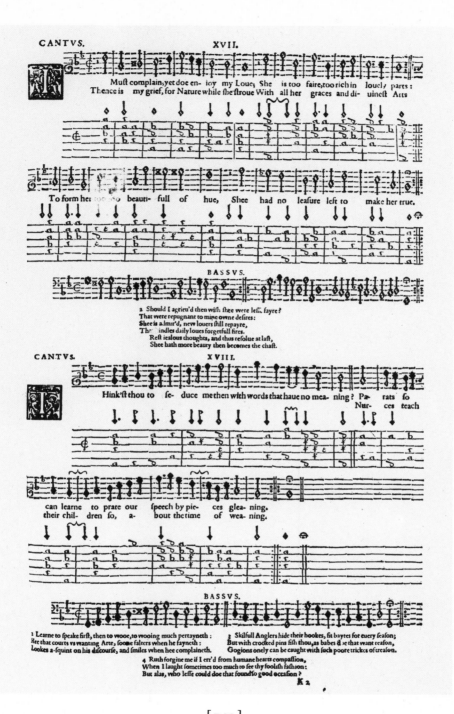

CANTVS.   XVII.

Must complain, yet doe en- ioy my Loue, She is too faire, too rich in louely parts :
Thence is my grief, for Nature while she stroue With all her graces and di- uinest Arts

To form her too- too beauti- full of hue, Shee had no leasure left to make her true.

BASSVS.

2 Should I agrieu'd then wish shee were less fayre?
That were repugnant to mine owne desires:
Shee is almur'd, new louers still repayre,
Th[..] indles daily loues forgetfull fires.
Rest iealous thoughts, and thus resolue at last,
Shee hath more beauty then becomes the chast.

CANTVS.   XVIII.

Hink'st thou to se- duce me then with words that haue no mea- ning ? Pa- rats so
Nur- ces teach

can learne to prate our speech by pie- ces glea- ning.
their chil- dren so, a- bout the time of wea- ning.

BASSVS.

1 Learne to speake first, then to wooe, to wooing much pertayneth :   3 Skilfull Anglers hide their hookes, fit baytes for euery season;
Hee that courts vs wanting Arte, soone falters when he sayneth :   But with crocked pins fish thou, as babes & ie that want reason,
Lookes a-squint on his discourse, and smiles when hee complaineth.   Gogions only can be caught with such poore trickes of reason.

4 Ruth forgiue me if I err'd from humane hearts compassion,
When I laught sometimes too much to see thy foolish fashion:
But alas, who lesse could doe that found so good occasion ?

                                                                                    K 2

INDEX TO SONGS

Numbers in italics refer to facsimile pages.

This book has been set, designed and printed under the supervision
of Martino Mardersteig at the Stamperia Valdonega in Verona,
Italy. The type is Bembo. The calligraphy for the scores is
by Edith McKeon Abbott and the engraving for the
title page is by Leo Wyatt. The deluxe edition,
limited to 250 copies, is printed on paper
manufactured by Cartiera Magnani.
APRIL MCMLXXIII